Fig. 6. UPPER DECK (E)

Fig. 7.
MIDDLE DECK (F)

BUILDING THE
TITANIC

Launch

OF

White Star Royal Mail Triple-Screw Steamer

"TITANIC"

At BELFAST,

Wednesday, 31st May, 1911, at 12-15 p.m.

Admit Bearer.

BUILDING THE
TITANIC

The Creation of History's Most Famous Ocean Liner

Rod Green

CARLTON
BOOKS

This is a Carlton book

First published in 2005 by
Carlton Books Limited
20 Mortimer Street
London W1T 3JW

3 5 7 9 10 8 6 4 2

A CIP catalogue record for this book is available from the British Library.

ISBN 978 1 84732 745 1

Editorial Manager: Lorna Russell
Picture Research: Sarah Edwards
Art Director: Lucy Coley
Design: Simon Wilder
Production: Lisa Moore

Printed and bound in Dubai

The publishers would like to thank the following sources for their kind permission to reproduce
the pictures in this book. The page numbers for each of the photographs are listed below,
giving the page on which they appear in the book and any location indicator (l-left, r-right)

Aquarius Collection: Rank: 149

Christies Images Ltd 1996: 14   623.8243

Corbis Images: Bettmann: 132-133, 135, 142; /CORBIS SYGMA: 69; /Hulton-Deutsch Collection: 118-119; /Todd
Gipstein: 83; /Ralph White: 110-11, 126-127; /Underwood & Underwood: 46, 68, 71

Fr Browne SJ Collection / Irish Picture Library: 60r, 63, 70, 72, 73, 78, 114, 121, 122, 123, 128, 132

Getty Images: Fox Photos: 30; /General Photographic Agency: 28, 140; /Henry Guttmann: 12; /J. A. Hampton:
24-25; /Hulton Archive: 8, 10, 19l, 20, 37l, 117, 134; /R. Lock/Fox Photos: 34-35; /London Express: 124; F. J.
Mortimer: 80; /Miguel Riopa/AFP: 158; /Sean Sexton: 44; /Time Life Pictures/Mansell: 6, 79; /Topical Press
Agency: 102, 131, 147; /Topical Press Agency/Hulton Archive: 106

Harland & Wolff Heavy Industries Ltd: 33, 37r, 39, 43, 50-51, 52, 53, 54- 55, 56-57, 59, 64, 65, 75, 82, 84-85, 86,
90, 91r, 95, 96-97, 98-99, 101, 105, 108-109, 144, 150, 150-151, 153, 155

Illustrated London News Picture Library: 16-17, 22-23

Mary Evans Picture Library: 11, 13, 19r, 27, 40-41, 66-67, 138-139

TopFoto.co.uk: 60l, 74, 76, 136, 138, 141

Harland & Wolff Collection at Ulster Folk & Transport Museum: 2, 58, 66, 88-89, 91l, 92-93, 94, 120

Every effort has been made to acknowledge correctly and contact the source and/or copyright
holder of each picture and Carlton Books Limited apologises for any unintentional errors
or omissions that will be corrected in future editions of this book.

CONTENTS

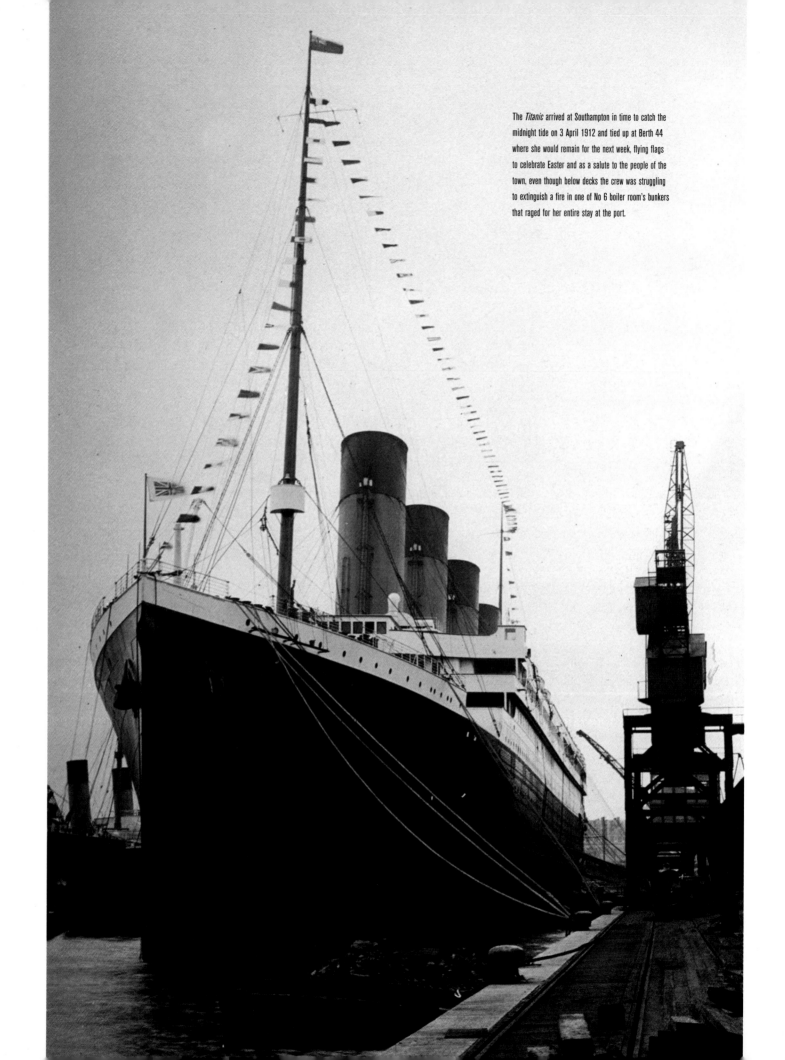

The *Titanic* arrived at Southampton in time to catch the midnight tide on 3 April 1912 and tied up at Berth 44 where she would remain for the next week, flying flags to celebrate Easter and as a salute to the people of the town, even though below decks the crew was struggling to extinguish a fire in one of No 6 boiler room's bunkers that raged for her entire stay at the port.

INTRODUCTION

Ask anyone on the streets of a major city anywhere in the world – London, New York, Paris, Tokyo, Sydney – to name a famous ship and the answer you are most likely to hear (providing you immediately discount the *Star Ship Enterprise*) is the *Titanic*. The multitude of books, films and TV specials about the sinking of the *Titanic* means that most of those people on the streets will be able to tell you that the world's most luxurious liner struck an iceberg and sank carrying some of the richest (and poorest) people ever to cross the Atlantic. They may even be able to tell you that the disaster happened during her maiden voyage, but ask them when it happened and you will hear guesses of anywhere from the late 19th century up to the beginning of the Second World War. I know – I've asked around. Not quite as far afield as New York and Tokyo, but enough people from enough places to realise that, while people know the legend of the *Titanic's* short life, they don't really know the story of the *Titanic*. While so many know a little about her demise, relatively few know the story of the *Titanic's* birth in the Belfast shipyard of Harland & Wolff; yet the story of the building of the *Titanic* is integral to that of her tragic destruction.

The *Titanic* was launched in 1912, the year when, in America, William Taft was replaced by Woodrow Wilson as President, and Arizona and New Mexico became states, bringing the total of the United States up to 48. In Britain, Herbert Asquith was Prime Minister and Captain Scott raced Amundsen to the South Pole. King George V was on the throne, speaking English with a pronounced German accent and retaining the family name of Saxe-Coburg-Gotha, despite ever worsening relationships between both Britain and Germany, and King George and his cousin the Kaiser. While war was brewing in Europe, so too was the situation in Ireland sliding inevitably towards armed conflict. The country was divided along religious and political lines, between Protestants and Catholics, loyalists and republicans. The *Titanic*, hailed as a modern-day marvel, was created in a country riven by strife that dated back centuries.

The *Titanic* could be described as a bridge between two different ages. She was the most modern ship afloat with radio, electric lighting, elevators, a fully-equipped gymnasium, a swimming pool and the most up-to-date safety features such as automatic watertight doors. Despite this, her basic construction involved as much brute force as it did finely calculated engineering. Welding was an art that had yet to catch on, so the *Titanic's* hull plates were held together with rivets that were hammered into place when red-hot, the plates overlapping like tiles on a house roof. She was built to a grand scale – the largest vessel afloat – but she was built using basic techniques that had changed very little since the construction of the first iron-hulled ships more than half a century earlier, even though the *Titanic* was ten times the size of those early ships. Furthermore, her up-to-date safety features were to prove woefully inadequate. The building of the *Titanic* taught the world fewer lessons than did her sinking.

Despite the shortcomings of her design and construction, none of which would have become apparent had she not struck the iceberg, the building of the *Titanic* was something of which the people of Belfast were, and still are, justifiably proud. The creation of the *Titanic* and her sister ship, the *Olympic*, was an immense achievement, showing that British ships were the most advanced in the world and that Belfast-built ships were the best. That the ship sank after hitting the iceberg (no other ship of the time would have survived such a trauma, either) could not detract from the quality of the craftsmanship that had gone into creating her sumptuous interiors. The luxury of the first-class fittings equalled the standard of the most expensive hotels in London or New York. A journalist from the *Southampton Times and Hampshire Express* who paid a visit to the *Titanic* in Southampton compared the *Titanic* with her sister ship, the *Olympic*, and noted: 'One person said that the *Olympic* was all that could be desired, and the *Titanic* was something even beyond that!'

Why such luxury? Why such a size? Why was such a ship built at this time? The story of the *Titanic's* sinking is an enthralling tale, but the story of the building of the *Titanic* has a fascination all of its own.

New York's Ellis Island immigration facility opened in 1891 with the potential to process up to 7,000 new arrivals every day. In 1907, shortly after this photograph was taken, 1.25 million people entered America via Ellis Island.

WHY BUILD

THE TITANIC?

When RMS *Titanic* set sail from Southampton on Wednesday 10 April 1912, she was not only the largest ship afloat, she was also officially the largest moving man-made object the world had ever seen. She was 882 feet (269 metres) long and weighed over 46,000 tons, so manoeuvring the giant ship was a delicate business. Six powerful tugs were required to push, pull and generally shepherd her away from the quayside out into position in the River Test, where she could finally engage her engines to begin making headway under her own steam.

As she picked up speed in the narrow channel, the *Titanic* passed two other liners docked side-by-side at berths 38 and 39 – the *Oceanic* and the *New York*. The *New York* was in the 'outside' berth closest to the *Titanic*. Built in 1888 on the Clyde, the *New York* was one of the finest liners of her day having won the prestigious Blue Riband award for the fastest crossing of the Atlantic in 1892, but she was no match for the *Titanic*. The new liner was over 350 feet (106 metres) longer than the *New York* and more than four times her tonnage, a difference in size that was to cause an immense problem as *Titanic* powered past.

The surge of the *Titanic's* wash created waves that flung the *New York* up and down with such violence that her six mooring lines snapped like threads. The *New York*, now floating free and unmanned save for a handful of workmen, was then drawn toward the *Titanic's* stern as helpless as a scrap of driftwood. A collision seemed inevitable and the crowds that had gathered to cheer the *Titanic's* departure, as well as many of those on the deck of the giant liner, could hardly believe their eyes. They had come to watch the greatest ship ever built depart on her maiden voyage; instead, it seemed as though they were about

to witness an embarrassing fiasco. The master of one of the *Titanic's* tugs, Captain Gale of the *Vulcan*, managed to throw a line to the *New York* but it, too, snapped. A second line was made fast by the workmen aboard the *New York* and it held, allowing the *Vulcan* to bring the *New York* under control when she was just 4 feet (1.2 metres) from the *Titanic*. Disaster was narrowly averted and the *Titanic* continued on her way to her first port of call at Cherbourg.

Given subsequent events, people could be forgiven for thinking that it might actually have been better for the *New York* to have made contact with the *Titanic*. A slow-speed collision would have caused relatively minor damage, but the *Titanic's* departure would have been delayed while repairs were made, and she might not then have come to grief four days later in mid-Atlantic. While the collision between the *New York* and the *Titanic* was narrowly avoided, how had the situation come about in the first place? Shouldn't the pilot who was aboard the *Titanic* directing her out of Southampton – as well as the

Right: The White Star Line became a major player in modern shipping with the launch of the *Oceanic* in 1870. Hailed as the world's first superliner, *Oceanic* was an innovative design, combining the hull and the superstructure rather than having the superstructure 'bolted on' to the hull. She also had running water in every cabin.

Far right: The first scheduled transatlantic steam ship passenger service was established in 1838 when Isambard Kingdom Brunel's *Great Western* took 14 days 12 hours to make the first of more than 70 Atlantic crossings.

Titanic's own officers and the harbour authorities – have foreseen the problem of the huge liner disturbing the *New York* and the *Oceanic* as she swept past? Perhaps this was because a similar situation had not arisen when the *Titanic* docked in Southampton six days earlier and the *New York* and *Oceanic* were tied up at berths 38 and 39 then, too. Perhaps no one had quite enough experience in dealing with a ship the size of the *Titanic*. She did, after all, dwarf the *New York*, a ship that, despite having been built 24 years earlier, still had ten years of working life ahead of her. But if the *New York* was still capable of operating as a transatlantic liner, why did the *Titanic* have to be so much bigger? Why had she been built to such a grand scale? Why, indeed, had the *Titanic* ever been built at all? The answer involves money, profit, pride, prestige and international rivalry.

On 1 January 1891, 15-year-old Annie Moore from County Cork in Ireland earned herself a shiny, new American $10 gold piece by becoming the first immigrant to pass through the Federal Bureau of Immigration's brand new receiving station at Ellis Island, New York. Annie and her two brothers were three of over 700 immigrants who arrived that first day on the SS *Nevada*, SS *City of Paris* and SS *Victory*. If handling an army of 700 new arrivals seems like a daunting task, bear in mind that Ellis Island was designed to receive up to 7,000 immigrants per day. New York was the main port of entry for the vast majority of immigrants searching for a new life in America, although ships carrying would-be Americans also sailed into Boston, Philadelphia, Baltimore, San Francisco, Savannah, Miami and New Orleans. Fleeing from poverty and starvation during the potato famine of 1845–50, Irish immigrants had headed west across the ocean in their thousands, making the Irish the largest single immigrant group in the United States.

But it wasn't just the Irish who were heading west. In the 1850s around 2.5 million people had travelled to America, almost a million of them coming from Germany and Eastern

Europe, where they were leaving behind poor harvests, or political or religious persecution. After the end of the American Civil War in 1865, the number of immigrants heading for New York grew from a steady flow to an unstoppable flood. During the 1870s there were 11.5 million immigrants to America, boosting the US population to 50 million and making New York the first state with more than five million inhabitants. This dramatic increase in the number of immigrants was not due solely to the ending of the Civil War. There was another factor that had a far greater influence than the end of the war. What affected the rate of immigration more than anything else was the coming of the age of steam.

In 1869 America's transcontinental railroad was completed when the Union Pacific and Central Pacific companies' tracks were linked at a ceremony at Promontory Point in Utah. Steam trains could now cross the country from coast to coast, cutting the New York to San Francisco journey time from three months to just eight days. America's vast hinterland was opening up in a way that had never been possible in the days of the wagon train and settlers were being encouraged to move inland from the coasts with the lure of free land for farming out in the 'prairie lands'.

A number of important pieces of legislation, including the Homestead Act of 1862, had been introduced to galvanise the population of rural America. Under the Homestead Act, a settler over the age of 21 could stake a claim to a parcel of land of up to 160 acres (65 hectares). In this way, around 270 million acres (109 million hectares), roughly 10 per cent of the United States, was handed over to small farmers. The railroad companies, with their ever-expanding rail network, mounted poster campaigns and placed advertisements to market themselves as the ideal means of escaping to this emergent Nirvana. But while they could certainly disperse the tide of immigrants efficiently cross-country, steam trains were not what delivered the new arrivals to America. Steam ships were responsible for that.

The first crossing of the Atlantic by a steam-powered ship was in 1819 when the SS *Savannah* sailed from Georgia to Liverpool, taking 23 days. The *Savannah's* voyage, however, did

Above: A Union Pacific Rail Road advertisement from 1869, the year in which lines from the east and west coasts met up in Utah to complete the transcontinental railroad. Passengers could now travel from New York to San Francisco in eight days instead of three months and could now reach the coast in 'less than four days' from mid-west cities such as Omaha.

Opposite: While the White Star Line was keen to grab its fair share of the immigrant trade, there were huge profits to be made from carrying wealthier passengers who not only paid huge sums for luxury suites on board, but also spent lavishly on fine wines and *à la carte* dining on board. This early advertising poster is clearly aimed at the more sophisticated traveller.

not immediately consign the fleets of transatlantic sailing ships to the breakers' yards as her crossing was regarded as something of a novelty and she still used sails for part of the journey. The first scheduled transatlantic passenger service by steam ship came in 1838 when Isambard Kingdom Brunel's *Great Western* crossed in 14 days 12 hours. The *Great Western* would go on to make more than 70 Atlantic crossings. But like the *Savannah*, she was a paddle steamer and paddle

steamers were more at home in calmer river or coastal waters than in the storm-tossed Atlantic, where the rolling of the ship could lift the paddles – mounted on the sides of the ship – out of the water. Not only did the consequent noise and vibration give cause for concern among the passengers but, with no water to push against, the exposed paddle wheel would race faster and faster, a situation that could easily result in serious damage to the machinery.

A greater problem in the early days of the steam ship, however, was the inefficiency of the engines. Steam engines used a huge amount of wood or coal – more than could sensibly be carried for a long journey. This problem was solved, in part, by Brunel who would go on to prove his theory that steam-powered ships could be built bigger and carry more coal when he launched the *Great Britain.* At 322 feet (98 metres) long, she was the largest vessel afloat – 100 feet (30 metres) longer than any other ship. Bigger ships, along with huge improvements in the efficiency of steam engines, provided a tantalising prospect for the owners of shipping lines.

The new steam ships cut the Atlantic crossing from the five or six weeks taken by a sailing ship, to just 11 days when Samuel Cunard's *Britannia* made the journey in 1840. Steam ships were not reliant on the wind and could be expected to arrive in port at or around the scheduled time. They were also bigger and could carry far more passengers – the few dozen passengers on an average sailing ship became a few hundred on a steam ship. By the time Brunel's *Great Britain* dispensed with paddles and became the first iron-hulled, screw-propeller-driven ship to cross the Atlantic in 1843, the way ahead was clear. Steam ships were going to become, bigger, better and faster.

By the early 1870s, over 95 per cent of the passengers arriving in New York disembarked from a steam ship. Dozens of small steamship companies sprang up with, among others, the Hamburg-America Line, Holland-America Line, Leyland Line, Dominion Line, White Star Line, Red Star Line, Cunard Line and Inman Line all criss-crossing the Atlantic in competition with each other for freight and passengers. It seemed as though there was plenty of trade for all, with a massive increase in

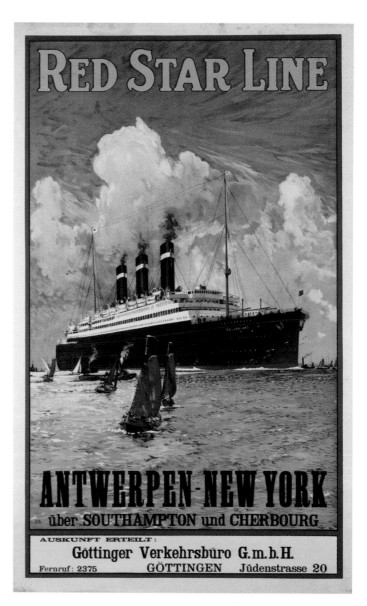

Above: The International Navigation Company, the American conglomerate backed by J P Morgan that became the International Mercantile Marine Company in 1902, was perhaps better known as the Red Star Line. Although founded in Philadelphia in 1871, the Red Star Line was registered in Belgium under a subsidiary company and sailed to New York and Philadelphia via Southampton and Cherbourg from 1873. The Red Star Line finally disappeared when the company ceased trading in 1934.

cargo from America – principally cotton, tobacco and wheat – and a blossoming trade in passenger traffic throughout the second half of the nineteenth century. The competition for business, however, coupled with a downturn in the American economy in 1873 that would be repeated again ten years later and yet again ten years after that, meant that many of the new companies struggled to make a sufficient profit. Ships changed hands or were leased between companies and amalgamations became inevitable, especially when American financier John Pierpont Morgan decided to take an interest in shipping.

J P Morgan's interest was inspired by two American ship owners: Clement Griscom and Bernard Baker. Griscom owned the America Line and was also involved with the International Navigation Company of Philadelphia which, in turn, had a major stake in the Red Star Line. Baker owned the Atlantic Transport Line and in 1896 he also acquired the National Line operating out of Liverpool. Around the same time, Griscom took over the Inman Line of Liverpool. Both Griscom and Baker were keen to continue expanding their shipping interests. For Griscom this meant seeking finance from the Philadelphia bankers Drexel & Co (who had close links to the Morgan Bank in New York) to fund the building of six new ships. Baker, on the other hand, considered selling his Atlantic Transport Line (ATL) to the British-owned Leyland Line, one of the biggest cargo shippers involved in the Atlantic routes. Griscom eventually persuaded Baker that the best way forward for themselves and the future of American merchant shipping was to pool their resources. Baker's ATL merged with Griscom's International Navigation Company and the finance originally sought by Griscom now came from J P Morgan. The finance was not, however, simply for six new ships. In a surprising turn of events the new conglomerate made some aggressive moves (generally attributed to J P Morgan), quickly acquiring the cargo-carrying Leyland Line, the Dominion Line and the prestigious White Star Line.

By 1902 the International Navigation Company, soon to change its name to the International Mercantile Marine Company (IMMC), was one of the most important shipping organisations operating in the North Atlantic. With J P Morgan's help, Griscom and Baker, who had been the only American ship owners competing for transatlantic business, had created a force to be reckoned within the IMMC. Their ships sailed under the flags of three different nations: the United States, Belgium (the Red Star Line ships had been sailing from Antwerp to Philadelphia and New York since 1873 and were registered in Belgium under a subsidiary company) and Great Britain. The National Line, Inman, Leyland, Dominion and White Star Lines were all British, operating British-built ships registered in the UK and flying the British flag.

The fact that so much American-owned shipping was in foreign hands was more than just an annoyance to J P Morgan and his IMMC partners. When competing for the contract to carry the US Mail in 1891, the best and fastest ships of the International Navigation Company fleet were the Inman Line's *City of New York* and *City of Paris*. The government contract required that the US Mail be carried on ships capable of maintaining at least 20 knots on the Atlantic crossing between New York and Southampton. For carrying the mail, the US government offered a subsidy grant of eight dollars per mile. The only drawback was that the *City of New York* and the *City of Paris* had to be re-registered as the *New York* and the *Paris* to sail under the American flag. The flag transfer was duly completed in 1892, but there were many who were unhappy about the prospect of what were seen as British assets being sold off to the Americans. By the time the IMMC bought the White Star Line in 1902, what was perceived as the gradual seepage of British merchant shipping into American hands caused an uproar in the British press. The White Star Line's great competitor, the Cunard Line, was also in J P Morgan's sights, but the British government took swift steps to ensure that Cunard remained wholly British.

Morgan's response was to step up the price war that the IMMC had instigated. He acquired a controlling interest in the Holland-America Line through a consortium formed with the major German lines, Hamburg-America and Norddeutscher-Lloyd. Morgan's aim in forming the consortium was not only to control prices on the transatlantic route, but also to rationalise shipping schedules to ensure that New York, for example, did

THE GROWTH OF THE ATLANTIC GREYHOUNDS

The First Cunarder, "Britannia" (1840)

This was one of the four vessels with which the Cunard line started ; 207 ft. long, 1,154 tons, 740 h.p., speed 8¼ knots ; took 12 days 10 hr. to cross the Atlantic in 1840

The diagrams give a striking impression of the growth of the transatlantic vessels which have brought England and America into such close touch. Starting from the "Savannah" of 100 ft. and 350 tons, which took 29½ days to cross over, we have reached the colossal "Mauretania," which is 787 ft. long and has a gross tonnage of 32,500, and will cross the Atlantic in less than a fifth of the time which was possible in 1819, when the "Savannah" essayed the task. Although the "Savannah" was the first steamship to cross the Atlantic she did not complete the voyage entirely under steam, her paddle-wheels being stowed on

SAVANNAH   GREAT WESTERN   BRITANNIA

SIRIUS

OREGON   UMBRIA & ETRURIA   CITY OF PARIS

CAMPANIA & LUCANIA   KAISER WILHELM II.

		Length ft.	Gross Tonnage				Length ft.	Gross Tonnage
1819	SAVANNAH	100	350		1874	BRITANNIC	455	5,004
1837	GREAT WESTERN	212	1,340		1883	OREGON	500	7,375
1837	SIRIUS	178	703		1884	AMERICA	432	6,500
1840	BRITANNIA	207	1,154		1884	UMBRIA	501·6	7,718
1861	SCOTIA	366	3,870		1888	CITY OF PARIS	560	10,499

The White Star Liner, "Britannic" (1874)

Built in Belfast ; 455 ft. long, 5,004 tons, 5,000 h.p., speed 16 knots ; quickest passage 7½ days

The Turbine Cunarder, "Lusitania" (1

Built by Brown at Clydebank ; 787·6 ft. long, 32,500 tons, 65,000 h.p., speed 25 knots ; carries 50

The Guion Liner, "Oregon" (1883)

Built on the Clyde ; 500 ft. long, 7,375 tons, 7,375 h.p., speed 18·3 knots

The Cunard Liner, "Umbria" (1884)

Built on the Clyde ; 501·6 ft. long, 7,718 tons, 15,000 h.p., speed 20 knots ; carries 400 first, 200 second, and 500 third class passengers

The American Liner, "Philadelphia" (1888)

Built on the Clyde ; 527·6 ft. long, 10,499 tons, 20,000 h.p., speed 20½ knots ; carries 400 first and 250 second class passengers

The

Built at Belfast ; 565·8

... during the greater part of the run. The first ship which crossed entirely under steam was the ...yal William," built at Quebec. The honour of beginning the great Atlantic ferry rests with the ...ius," a small ship of 703 tons. She arrived at New York in 1838 after an eventful voyage a few ...s ahead of a rival—the "Great Western." Shortly after leaving port the crew of the "Sirius" ...sed to proceed in her, declaring it was unsafe to continue the voyage in so small a ship, and but ...he energy and determination of her commander, backed by firearms, she would doubtless have put ... Eventually she arrived safely at her destination after a passage of about eighteen days

SCOTIA   BRITANNIC & GERMANIC

...f NEW YORK   TEUTONIC & MAJESTIC

LUSITANIA & MAURETANIA

	Length ft.	Gross Tonnage
TEUTONIC	565·8	9,984
CAMPANIA	600	12,950
KAISER WILHELM II.	706·5	20,000
KAISERIN AUGUSTE VICTORIA	690	14,350
LUSITANIA	787·6	32,500

The Cunarder, "Scotia" (1861)

Built (of iron) on the Clyde; 366 ft. long, 3,870 tons, 4,200 h.p. She was described at the time as "the champion and model of a mercantile ocean steamship"

The Norddeutscher Lloyd, "Kaiser Wilhelm II." (1903)

Built at Stettin; 706·5 ft. long, 20,000 tons, 40,000 h.p., speed 23·58 knots; carries 775 first, 343 second, and 770 third class passengers

The Norddeutscher Lloyd, "Kaiser Wilhelm der Grosse" (1897)

Built at Stettin; 648·6 ft. long, 14,350 tons, 28,000 h.p., speed 23 knots; carries 400 first and 205 second class passengers

...econd class passengers

...tar Liner, "Teutonic" (1889)

...tons, 16,000 h.p., speed 20 knots; carries 300 first and 190 second class passengers

The Cunarder, "Campania" (1893)

Built on the Clyde; 600 ft. long, 12,950 tons, 28,000 h.p., speed 22 knots; carries 400 first and 300 second and 600 third class passengers

DRAWN BY A. B. CULL

Left: Isambard Kingdom Brunel proved that steamships would operate more efficiently and more cost-effectively the bigger they became. This illustration shows how ship design changed and how quickly the steam ships grew in size from the first ones to cross the Atlantic – the *Savannah*, *Great Western* and *Britannia* to the *Lusitania* and *Mauretania*.

not see three different ships from three different lines all leaving for England on the same day. These three ships would have advertised and competed for the same cargoes and passengers. Common sense held that it would be better for business to have the three ships leave on different days. In fact, it would be ideal if a major liner could leave New York *every* day carrying cargo, passengers and mail. In driving down the price of a third-class passage to America – at one point to as little as £2 – Morgan hoped to create a virtual monopoly in the North Atlantic. The only major fly in the ointment was Cunard.

Born in Halifax, Nova Scotia, in 1787, the son of a timber merchant, Samuel Cunard had an entrepreneurial flair that saw him managing his own general store at the age of 17. He later joined his father in the timber business, but he harboured far more wide-ranging ambitions. He soon had the Cunard family involved in coal, iron, whaling and shipping. Before he had reached the age of 30 he was running a shipping line with around 40 vessels and he would go on to become one of the most influential men in Nova Scotia. Cunard had amassed a considerable personal fortune by the time he crossed the Atlantic in 1838 to enter into negotiations for the lucrative transatlantic mail contract about to be offered for tender by Her Majesty's government. As the contract was for a steamship service, Cunard formed the British and North American Royal Mail Steam Packet Company – despite not owning a single steamship. Cunard won the contract partly by promising that he would guarantee regular sailings throughout the year, including the unpredictably stormy winter months. Mindful of the swingeing penalties for failing to maintain a regularly scheduled, punctual service, other shipping magnates with whom he was in competition shied away.

Cunard's first steamship, the paddle steamer *Britannia*, crossed the Atlantic from Liverpool to Boston in 1840, albeit with its steam engines augmented by a substantial array of sails. Thereafter, Cunard expanded his shipping line with the addition of, among others, his first iron-hulled, screw-propeller-driven ship, the *Andes*, in 1852. Samuel Cunard was knighted by Queen Victoria for his services to the British maritime industry in 1859, and died six years later in 1865.

The Cunard Line, as his shipping company was then known, grew to become the most innovative and respected shipping line in the world, being the first to introduce electric lighting and wireless communications on board its ships. By 1870, when the White Star Line (which had previously traded on the Australian route with wooden-hulled sailing vessels) launched the iron-hulled *Oceanic,* built specifically for service as a passenger liner in the North Atlantic, Cunard was operating around two dozen cargo and passenger vessels on the North Atlantic as well as in the Mediterranean. Cunard's dominant position on the transatlantic route was, however, far from unassailable. Within the space of a year, White Star was to follow the 3,707-ton *Oceanic* with her sister ships the *Atlantic*, *Baltic* and *Republic*. The following year came the larger *Celtic* and *Adriatic*, and by 1875 there were a dozen White Star liners. Not all of these were intended exclusively for the North Atlantic – White Star also sailed to the Middle East, India, the Far East and Australia – but two in particular provided serious competition for Cunard. The *Britannic* and *Germanic* could both maintain 16 knots, a speed that allowed them to cross the Atlantic in comfortably less than eight days. The time taken to cross the Atlantic was fast becoming a hotly contested issue.

The much-coveted Blue Riband, an honour for which the different shipping lines competed, allowed the ship that achieved the fastest crossing of the Atlantic to fly a blue pennant from her mast. The ship that held the Blue Riband and the shipping line that owned the Blue Riband holder earned themselves a great deal of publicity. It was a matter of immense pride and huge prestige to be able to market the ship or company that provided the fastest passage across the Atlantic. The little blue pennant fluttering from the masthead, therefore, represented hard currency – dollars and cents, pounds and shillings – in ticket revenue from passengers who wanted to sail on the fastest liner afloat, and in cargo revenue from exporters who needed to get their goods across the water by the quickest means possible.

Cunard had first held the Blue Riband as early as 1840 when the *Britannia* crossed from New York at an average speed of just over 10 knots, a journey time of just under ten days. At

Far left: Sir Samuel Cunard was an entrepreneur from Canada who, in 1838, won the contract to provide a transatlantic steamship service carrying the Royal Mail despite the fact that, at that time, he did not own even one steamship. Cunard was knighted by Queen Victoria in 1859 and died in 1865 at the age of 78.

Left: Born into a banking family in Hartford, Connecticut, in 1837, J P Morgan became the most powerful financier in America, leading a group that saved the US government from bankruptcy in 1895 and preventing a Wall Street crash in 1907. He died in 1913.

that time, the Blue Riband may not have meant quite as much as it did 20 years later, when steam was completely overpowering sail and the Atlantic waters were churning with competition on scheduled steamship services. By then, the Blue Riband was a trophy to be flown in the face of the opposition, a banner to wave that said you were the fastest and the best – and you had proved it. Different records were set and broken for both east and westbound crossings, but a glance at the history of the westbound Blue Riband shows how keenly contested it was. Although the honour changed hands several times up to 1856, Cunard held it from then, through the efforts of the *Persia* and the *Scotia*, up to 1872, when the new White Star liner *Adriatic* achieved an average speed of over 14.5 knots – a crossing time just a few minutes short of eight days. Three years later, White Star's *Germanic* took the average speed up to 14.65 knots and, although Inman Lines' *City of Berlin* briefly took the record in 1875, White Star retained the honour through *Britannic* and *Germanic* for the next six years.

In 1882 another British company, the Guion Line, was able to offer its passengers the fastest Atlantic crossing on its steamers the *Alaska* and *Oregon*. Guion's ships took the crossing time to under seven days for the first time, with the *Oregon* raising the average speed to 18.56 knots. The *Oregon* was sold to Cunard in 1884, the same year that Cunard's

Etruria made the crossing at 18.73 knots in just 6 days $5^1/2$ hours. The *Etruria* broke her own record in 1888 with an average speed of 19.56 knots and, along with her sister ship, the *Umbria*, held the Blue Riband until 1889, when the Inman Lines' *City of Paris* took the crossing time to under six days. Inman Lines was by this time known as Inman & International and was part of the American International Navigation Company. However, the *City of Paris* was still operating under a British flag when she broke her own record and raised the average speed for a crossing from Queenstown in Ireland to a fraction over 20 knots. In 1891 White Star's *Majestic* and *Teutonic* achieved average speeds of 20.1 and 20.35 knots, making the crossing from Queenstown in just 5 days, 16 hours and 35 minutes. The *City of Paris* snatched the record back in 1892, but Cunard reclaimed the title when the *Campania* and *Lucania* took the average speed up to just under 22 knots in 1893, maintaining their position as the fastest transatlantic liners for the next five years. It was then that the unthinkable happened.

Being forced to relinquish the Blue Riband now and again to one of the other British lines wasn't a position Cunard relished, but at least the trophy was being held safe in British hands. Other Blue Riband liners flew the Union Jack just as the Cunarders did and sharing the honour with other British-built ships showed that Queen Victoria's empire was sustained by the finest merchant navy in the world. British technology and British engineering produced the fastest, most advanced ships on the high seas. Truly, Britannia ruled the waves. The Germans, however, had other ideas.

In November 1897 the Norddeutscher-Lloyd (NDL) liner *Kaiser Wilhelm der Grosse* set a new record average speed of 22.33 knots for an eastbound crossing and four months later took the westbound record at 22.29 knots. For the first time since the *Great Western* made the crossing 60 years before, the Blue Riband flew from the mast of a ship that did not also fly the Union Jack. The British, who had prided themselves on being the world's foremost maritime nation for centuries, took it as a huge affront to national pride that the Blue Riband had been lost to the Germans. Cunard was especially aggrieved. The Cunarders could be forgiven for having come to believe that the Blue Riband rightfully belonged to them alone. They had held the record for no less than 25 of the previous 42

years. But the *Kaiser Wilhelm* wasn't only proclaiming its superiority in terms of speed. NDL advertised it as the largest ship afloat, at almost 1,000 tons more than the *Lucania* and 20 feet (6 metres) longer. Despite being bigger, she carried almost 250 fewer passengers – 800 third class (or 'steerage'), 370 second class and 590 first class. This also led to NDL claiming that the *Kaiser Wilhelm* was the most spacious and luxurious liner in the world, a claim that was backed up by the acres of polished wood and sumptuous furnishings.

While providing a demeaning slap in the face for Cunard, the *Kaiser Wilhelm* also demonstrated how ships were becoming bigger as well as faster. Compared with Cunard's *Etruria*, launched just 12 years previously, the *Kaiser Wilhelm* had a displacement that was 6,000 tons greater, was over 100 feet longer and could accommodate more than 400 extra passengers. Brunel's *Great Britain* of 1843, once the largest ship afloat, had been just 3,200 tons, carrying only 120 first class and 132 second class passengers. Brunel's idea, however, that steamships would provide economies of scale, with bigger most definitely meaning better, was now being proved beyond a shadow of a doubt.

The Hamburg-America Line, also known as Hapag, shared in Germany's glory when their liner *Deutschland* increased the average speed for a westbound Atlantic crossing to just over 23 knots in 1900. The *Deutschland* lost the title to NDL's *Kronprinz Wilhelm* in 1902, but grabbed it back in 1903. The Germans were to hold on to the Blue Riband for the next four years until the arrival of a ship that heralded a whole new breed of superliner.

Britain sailed into the twentieth century with its domination of the North Atlantic passenger trade routes under serious threat. Not only were the Germans crossing the Atlantic faster, but many of Britain's finest ships were no longer actually British. In 1902 J P Morgan's IMMC bought the Leyland Line for $11 million, the Dominion Line for $4.5 million and the White Star Line for $32 million. Today this would represent an investment of many billions of dollars – the sort of investment that sends shock waves through the stock markets and forces governments to take an interest. Takeovers on this scale can affect people's livelihoods, the shape of an industry, the economy of the country and politicians' jobs. More than that, for an island nation such as Great Britain shipping is its lifeline to the outside world and in times of war the merchant marine plays a vital role as part of the military. At the time of the Crimean War in 1853 most of Cunard's fleet was commandeered by the British Admiralty to be used as troop ships and both Cunard and White Star liners were used to ferry troops to and from South Africa during the Boer War of 1899–1902. For future emergencies, the Admiralty needed to rely on being able to requisition ships flying the British flag, operated by British companies and with British crews. The potential for disastrous

security breaches and the infiltration of spies and saboteurs if too many foreigners were involved was obvious.

There was also another military factor to be taken into consideration. The new German ships had the potential to be converted in time of war into armed cruisers capable of causing havoc among merchant vessels or supply convoys, and able to outrun most naval vessels. The Royal Navy's most advanced warship, HMS *Bellerophon*, due to be launched in 1907, was not expected to achieve more than 21 knots. The Royal Navy had to show that it could counter the threat posed by the German liners by deploying its own armed cruisers if needs be. For economic and military reasons as well as national pride, therefore, the British Government and the Admiralty saw its close relationship with Cunard as being more valuable than ever before. Cunard, however, was embroiled in a vicious commercial battle with the IMMC, as J P Morgan was determined either to buy them out or wipe them out to achieve his goal of an Atlantic monopoly.

While trade agreements prevented the British government from stepping in to offer direct support to Cunard or to subsidise its commercial operations, in 1903 Cunard's chairman, Lord Inverclyde, put forward a proposal that would appeal to both the government and his company. To compete with the Germans and with the White Star Line, Inverclyde needed two new ships for Cunard – two new ships that were bigger, faster and more luxurious than anything ever built. All he needed from the government was a loan. The loan, however, had to be at a very special rate – 2.75 per cent over 20 years. It was also for a very special amount – £2.6 million. That may not sound like much for a government to spend nowadays but, 100 years later, at the beginning of the twenty-first century, a similar ship was built – the biggest, most luxurious, fastest, most expensive transatlantic liner in the world – the *Queen Mary 2*. The £2.6 million Lord Inverclyde asked for represents the cost of building today two *Queen Mary 2s*, at £550 million each. In return for the loan, Cunard would ensure that the vessels were made available to the Admiralty whenever they were required, to be used as armed cruisers, troop ships or hospital ships.

SECOND CLASS
SMOKE ROOM

2nd CLASS
PROMENADE
& LOUNGE

SECOND CABIN
DINING SALOON (ON
SALOON DECK)

VERANDAH
& CAFÉ

SALOON
SMOKE ROOM

SALOON LOUNGE
ROOM
1st C. DINING

BOAT DECK

PROMENADE
DECK

STEERING GEAR

FIREMEN'S QUARTERS

MAILS

FRESH WATER TANKS

GO AHEAD
TURBINE

ASTERN
TURBINE

ENGINES

STARTING
PLATFORM

MAIN DECK

100 FT.

Controversy and conspiracy theories still surround the sinking of the *Lusitania* by a German submarine during the First World War. She may have been secretly carrying ammunition supplied illegally by the then neutral United States. This could have made her a 'legitimate' target for the U-boat. Nevertheless, 1,200 passengers died in the tragedy.

MAIN STAIRCASE & ELEVATORS

1ˢᵗ CLASS NURSERY

WIRELESS

1ˢᵗ CLASS LIBRARY

OFFICERS' ROOMS

NAVIGATING BRIDGE

CAPTAIN'S ROOMS

BOAT DECK

PROMENADE DECK

UPPER DECK

SALOON DECK

MAIN DECK

LOWER DECK

BOILERS

COAL

REFRIGERATED

FRESH WATER

CARGO

CARGO

THE POINT AT WHICH THE TORPEDO STRUCK VESSEL

The Cunard liner *Carmania*, launched in 1905, was fitted with new turbine engines as an experiment. Her sister ship, *Caronia*, was fitted with traditional reciprocating engines. In service, *Carmania* was faster and burned less fuel, so the decision was taken that the next generation of Cunarders, *Lusitania* and *Mauretania*, should be turbine-powered.

The idea of the British government helping to fund the building of ships in return for the ships being called into service by the Admiralty in times of crisis was not a new one. The White Star liners *Teutonic* and *Majestic*, for example, had both been built with government grants 20 years before. It was the scale of Lord Inverclyde's proposal and the huge amount of money involved that made it so audacious.

The government agreed, but had a few stipulations to make. No doubt Lord Inverclyde had expected this. The Admiralty had always had certain requirements for mail ships, with which Cunard had been happy to comply. They had agreed, for example, that their mail ships' crews should include among their number at least one officer of the Royal Navy with the power to take over the ship to protect the Royal Mail should the need arise. In effect, most of the 'mail' officers were expected to do little more than enjoy the trip. The government's requirements for the new ships were extensive and precise, extending not only to the building and operating of the ships, but also to the running of the Cunard Line and all of its other ships.

The new ships had to be able to maintain an average speed in moderate weather of 24–25 knots and all plans and designs were to be subject to the approval of the Admiralty. Construction of the ships was to come under the scrutiny of an independent inspector to ensure that the specifications were being adhered to rigidly. In addition, provision had to be made for the installation of 'fittings' that would prepare the ships for military use, with storage provided for such fittings, and the stored fittings had to be properly maintained. Cunard further undertook to maintain a mail service once a week from Liverpool via Queenstown to New York, leaving on a Saturday, and promised that the usual provisions for facilities such as a mail sorting office would be made on any vessel used to carry the mail. They were not to supply any vessel on charter except to the Indian government, and none of the company's ships capable of 17 knots or more could be sold without the government's approval.

The agreement required that all of Cunard's vessels be kept seaworthy and ready for inspection, as all of them would be at the disposal of the Admiralty whenever they were required. All vessels had to be registered under a British flag, and all company steamship masters, officers and at least 75 per cent of the crew had to be British. The company as a whole had to remain under British control with all company directors and senior managers to be British, and no shares were to be sold to foreigners or foreign companies. And there was more – the clauses and sub-clauses covering Cunard's obligations under the agreement punctuated the contract like rivets on a ship's hull. Lord Inverclyde had avoided being boarded or sunk by the pirate J P Morgan; instead, he'd been press-ganged by the Navy. Taking the king's shilling, however, meant that Cunard could now begin work on building the world's most advanced ships.

Lord Inverclyde wanted the two new liners to enter service as quickly as possible, so the contracts for building the ships were awarded to two separate shipyards. The John Brown yard at Clydebank was chosen for the construction of the first ship, the *Lusitania*, while her sister ship, the *Mauretania*, was to be built in Newcastle by Swan, Hunter and Wigham Richardson. The ships' romantic names were exactly that – Roman. The *Lusitania* was named after Roman Portugal, and the *Mauretania* after Roman Morocco. That air of romance was also to be integral to the design of the ships' interiors, which were intended from the outset to be distinctly different, affording each ship its own individual character. (Exactly the opposite approach was adopted by the White Star Line when the *Olympic* and *Titanic* were fitted out a few years later, as they decided on a more uniform look that made both ships immediately identifiable as sisters.) Further adding to the differences between the new Cunarders, the shipyards competed with one another to add their own refinements, with the approval of the owners, each hoping to build the biggest, fastest and best of the sister ships.

The *Lusitania* was the first to be completed. Her keel plates were laid down in June 1904 and two years later she was ready for launch. She was over 785 feet (239 metres) long, more than 150 feet (45 metres) longer than the *Kaiser Wilhelm der Grosse*. Lady Inverclyde broke a bottle of Champagne over the *Lusitania's* bow, watched by around 20,000 spectators. Sadly,

Lord Inverclyde did not live to see the launch of his superliner – he died in 1905 when only 44 years of age. The *Lusitania* was to spend a further year being fitted out. She was divided into 34 separate watertight compartments, which were believed to make her virtually unsinkable, and had 192 furnaces to heat the 27 boilers that provided her steam power.

The steam, however, was not driving the normal type of reciprocating engine, but the largest steam turbines ever built. Instead of installing the conventional style of steamship engines, where steam from the boilers expands in giant pistons that pump up and down to turn a shaft (much as the pistons in a modern car engine do), Cunard decided to go for the new turbine designs. They had tested turbine engines in a smaller ship, the *Carmania*, which had been launched in 1905. The *Carmania's* sister ship, the *Caronia*, was fitted with traditional reciprocating steam 'piston' engines, and the performances of the two otherwise identical ships were compared. The *Carmania* was more efficient, using less fuel and achieving higher speeds than the *Caronia*. The decision was made. The new Cunarders would be fitted with turbine engines.

Turbines are engines where steam from the boilers is fed at high pressure over the blades of a turbine, forcing them to turn like the sails of a windmill and thus spin the propeller shaft. They were far more expensive to produce as they had to be built using more costly materials and highly advanced engineering technology. Nevertheless, the potential savings in fuel costs, the greater power output and resultant higher speed were well worth the initial investment. Theoretically, the smoother operation of the turbines' rotating motion transferring power to the spinning propeller shaft with greater ease than the reciprocal engines' pumping motion should have caused far less vibration throughout the ship and provided a more relaxing environment for the passengers.

Unfortunately, this was not the case in practice and, when the *Lusitania* set out on her sea trials, violent shuddering was experienced in her stern section at high speed. Her entire stern had to be gutted and fitted with extra bracing beams to try to counter the problem. The 142 second-class cabins were torn apart in the process, causing a delay in her completion of over a month.

Finally, she was handed over to Cunard, who opened her to the public in September 1907 in Southampton, allowing thousands of visitors to come aboard and marvel at the combination of craftsmanship and technology employed on the greatest ship afloat. The plasterwork, which was decorated with gold leaf that had been used by the designer James Millar to create a Georgian or Louis XVI-style interior décor in the public areas, was lit in breathtaking fashion by electric lights. Other electrical equipment such as elevators, fans and clocks were plugged into the *Lusitania's* 300 miles (483 kilometres) of electric wiring, giving the undeniable impression that this was a thoroughly modern ship; the classically carved oak chairs and tables might have graced the most elegant of London's finest hotels. The *Lusitania* was, in fact, a 31,550-ton floating hotel capable of accommodating over 2,000 guests. No lumbering giant, within a month of entering service *Lusitania* brought the Blue Riband back to Cunard. She subsequently lost it, but only to her sister ship, the *Mauretania*, who raised the average Atlantic crossing speed to 26 knots, cutting the journey time to just under four and a half days. It was a record the *Mauretania* would hold from 1909 until 1929. Sadly, the *Lusitania* was torpedoed by a German U-boat in 1915 and sank with the loss of almost 1,200 lives.

The *Lusitania* and *Mauretania* re-established

Left: Lord Inverclyde, chairman of the Cunard Line, was the driving force behind the unprecedented deal with the British government that saw his shipping company receive preferential loans for the building of the *Lusitania* and *Mauretania*. Unfortunately, he died in 1905 at the age of just 44, one year before *Lusitania's* launch.

Cunard as the leading shipping line in the North Atlantic. Not only had they produced the world's largest ships, showcasing the skills, ingenuity and technical prowess of British craftsmen as well as the superiority of British industry, they had humbled the haughty Germans into the bargain. With increasing political tension between the two nations, tension that would erupt into war seven years later, the Cunarders were lauded as national champions. The swell of nationalist fervour elevated the Cunard Line, in the eyes of the great patriotic British public, to the position of being 'Britain's' shipping line – the pride of the nation. But that pride was not necessarily shared by all of King Edward VII's subjects.

Belgrave Square in Knightsbridge is one of London's most exclusive addresses. Situated just a stone's throw from Hyde Park Corner and the gardens of Buckingham Palace, the elegant town houses were built on a former swamp that was drained and prepared for development by Thomas Cubbit in the early nineteenth century. The mews cottages tucked away in the side streets surrounding the square were once used as stabling and servants' quarters, while the grand buildings on the square itself are so big as to be impractical as private dwellings nowadays. Today, they have been taken over as the embassies of Germany, Spain, Portugal, Syria, Turkey as well as the Saudi Arabian consulate and institutions such as the Royal College of Psychiatrists. A century ago, however, Belgrave Square was home to London's social elite. The residents were among the wealthiest people in Britain, titled aristocrats who lived in great splendour.

On a mid-summer evening in 1907, Mr Joseph Bruce Ismay and his wife, Florence, arrived in the Square, having been invited to dinner at Downshire House, the London residence of Lord and Lady Pirrie. Lord Pirrie and Ismay were close business associates. Pirrie was the chairman of Harland & Wolff in Belfast, one of the largest shipbuilders in the world and Ismay the chairman of the White Star Line as well as president and managing director of the IMMC. Each had a vital financial interest in the other's business, which had led to all White Star Line ships being built in Belfast; each was also gravely concerned about the impact of the publicity that the new

Above: Part of Belgrave Square in London in the early 1900s. Most of the grand buildings were, at that time, private residences. A century later, the buildings have mostly been turned into embassies or institutions as their size and the cost of their upkeep make them impractical as modern family homes.

Cunarders, now nicknamed 'ocean greyhounds', were enjoying.

It was not considered to be good form to dwell on business matters at the dinner table, but afterwards the two had much to discuss. Ismay was determined that the White Star Line, long having prided itself on operating the finest ships of any transatlantic fleet and always providing its passengers with the ultimate in luxury travel, should not be openly relegated to the status of an 'also ran' in the eyes of the British public by the patriotic hysteria generated by the successes of the *Lusitania* and *Mauretania*. In Ismay's eyes, Cunard did not deserve to be regarded as the premier British shipping line – White Star ships still flew the Union Jack, after all, even though they were now owned by the IMMC and no longer as truly British as Cunard. The IMMC and J P Morgan had continued to run the shipping lines under subsidiary companies based in their home countries so that they could fly their own national flags and benefit from the national loyalties of passengers who wanted to travel on their own countries' ships. All of that loyalty and national pride now appeared to have been hijacked by Cunard. If things continued in this vein, it was easy to see how Cunard would come to be the principal player in transatlantic shipping.

Lord Pirrie, of course, fully understood how that situation would affect Harland & Wolff. A significant downturn in business for White Star would mean that new orders would dry up, spelling disaster for the Belfast shipyard. Although it might at first have seemed that the solution would be to cross the Atlantic faster than the Cunarders and take the Blue Riband from them, this was neither desirable nor practical. The pursuit of speed had never really been a priority for White Star. Elegance and luxury were their watchwords, and it had never been White Star's policy to conquer the Atlantic in terms of speed alone, despite the fact that they had held the Blue Riband on many occasions in the past. In any case, winning the Blue Riband from Cunard could never generate as much enthusiasm or fire the emotions of the British public to the extent that it had done when Cunard took the honour from the Germans. Practically, there was also a problem in going for speed. White Star's fastest ships, the *Teutonic*, *Oceanic* and *Adriatic* could only achieve 21 knots to the Cunarders 26. Adapting them to make them faster would mean reducing cargo and passenger space to install new equipment. That would never be financially viable.

Building a new liner that could compete was really the only option, but the only way to be sure of outstripping the 'greyhounds' was to build a ship with bigger, better, more powerful turbines than the Cunarders'. The more conventional type of reciprocating engine simply could not produce the same kind of performance. But new turbines could take years and enormous amounts of money to develop, money that might better be spent on other aspects of a new ship, especially as the two men would not benefit from the sort of deal the late Lord Inverclyde had struck with the government. During their lengthy discussion the two explored all of the avenues open to them, ultimately concluding that their most sensible route was to do what the White Star Line had always prided itself upon – be the best.

There was no real need to involve the White Star Line in a futile race for the Blue Riband; no need to stray from company policy in that respect. They would simply build the biggest, most luxurious, safest, most impressive ocean-going vessel the world had ever seen. They would build a ship that would be as graceful and elegant as the room in which they were sitting, but this would be beauty on a grand scale – a ship to be envied by shipping lines and maritime nations the world over. Naturally, it would have to earn its keep, but they had little doubt that they would be able to attract customers. The passenger trade across the Atlantic hadn't been so buoyant for years.

Toward the end of the nineteenth century, the Inman Line had sent over 3,000 agents into Europe to sell passages to the relatives of immigrants already in America and, by 1907, despite ever more stringent US government immigration restrictions, more immigrants than ever before entered America – 1.25 million through Ellis Island alone. These passengers did not travel in the most luxurious accommodation – they were third or 'steerage' class – but a full complement of third-class passengers at the right fare could pay for enough coal to take a liner to New York and back again. There was also the mail subsidy to consider. No deal could ever be as good as the one Cunard had secured, but there was still money to be made in transporting the Royal Mail. The new liner would carry a certain amount of cargo, too, but the real profit was to be earned from those most affluent of travellers who were able to afford the most exquisite accommodation, the most sumptuously appointed cabins, the most attentive service. Ismay and Pirrie had to make the new ship the only choice for the Edwardian super-rich.

With this plan, however, they would need at least two ships to maintain a proper transatlantic service – or why not three? That, after all, was how the *Teutonic*, *Adriatic* and *Oceanic* operated – a kind of Atlantic shuttle service. Ismay and Pirrie set to work sketching out some ideas on paper that very night. They produced some rough drawings of how the new ships might look, also deciding that they should have names to reflect their status as the mightiest liners ever built – the *Olympic*, *Titanic* and *Gigantic*.

Following the demise of the *Titanic*, shipbuilding at Harland & Wolff in Belfast might have been expected to be badly affected. On the contrary, the shipyard went on to build ever bigger and more modern vessels. The *Stirling Castle* is seen here in the dry dock in 1935.

WHO BUILT THE TITANIC?

Lord Pirrie took the concept sketches and design ideas roughed out by himself and Ismay to Belfast where a number of key men would turn their ideas into solid steel reality. People had been building ships of one kind or another around the shores of Belfast Lough for as long as men had lived there and even the 'modern' industry that Lord Pirrie knew could trace its history back almost 250 years. In all that time, nothing approaching the size of the new ships he now presented to his design team had ever been attempted, not even by the mighty Harland & Wolff.

The company's history stretched back to 1791 and the beginning of the modern era of shipbuilding in Belfast, when an enterprising Scottish shipbuilder named William Ritchie saw the work of the Belfast Harbour Commission in straightening the River Lagan. The modern port facilities that were planned seemed ideal for supporting a new business venture and Ritchie applied for permission to establish a boat repair yard. Before long, he was not only repairing boats but also building them and within 20 years he had expanded his company from a workforce of just ten men to well over 100. Ritchie's brother, Hugh, eventually set up another shipyard on the Lagan with his partner, Alastair McLaine, and in 1820 launched the very first Irish-built steamship, the *Belfast*. More shipyards were to follow until in 1851 the Harbour Commission gave permission for the development of a new site on Queen's Island.

The island had been formed when the Harbour Commission dug a 'canal' to cut out a bend in the river during their ongoing programme of improvement. Water still flowed round the shallow bend, isolating the land that was to become Queen's Island (later, the 'bend' would be filled in, making Queen's Island technically no longer an island). The first shipbuilder on Queen's Island was the small firm of Thompson & Kirwan, to be followed by another, two years later, when Robert Hickson established the first yard dedicated to the building of iron-hulled ships. Almost immediately Hickson advertised for a shipyard manager and the man who got the job was a young engineer named Edward James Harland.

Born in Scarborough in May 1831, Harland was the son of a doctor who took a keen interest in all things mechanical and who was happy for his son to become apprenticed at the

engineering works of Robert Stephenson in Newcastle-upon-Tyne. In 1851 Harland moved to Glasgow to work for J & G Thompson, who built marine engines. He spent two years there before moving back to Tyneside as a manager at the Thomas Toward yard. His return to Tyneside lasted only a year before he moved to Belfast at the age of 23 to become Robert Hickson's shipyard manager. The young Harland was given a rough ride in Belfast to begin with, having to deal with wage disputes, supply problems and general industrial unrest in a business that was far from flourishing. He needed help to get the business back on its feet and on the advice of an old friend, the German entrepreneur Gustav Schwabe (who had financial interests in shipping with the Bibby Line of Liverpool), Harland employed Schwabe's nephew, Gustav Wolff, as his assistant.

Gustav Wilhelm Wolff, born in Hamburg in November 1834, was the son of a German businessman. He began his education in Germany but was sent to Liverpool College at the age of 14, joining the Manchester engineering firm of Joseph Whitworth & Co. two years later as an apprentice. He also worked as an engineering draughtsman for another company before being hired by Harland in 1857. The two men worked hard to breathe new life into the business, but by 1858 it was clear that Hickson wanted to bow out of shipbuilding and he offered to sell the entire yard to Harland for £5,000.

Again, seeking the advice of his old friend, Harland discussed the offer with Gustav Schwabe, who not only encouraged him to take the offer, but also provided the finance to make it possible for Harland to buy out Hickson. Gustav Wolff then proved his worth not only as a draughtsman and manager but also as a businessman when he was instrumental in securing an order from the Bibby Line for three new ships. The new liners were to be called the *Venetian*, *Sicilian* and *Syrian*. Launched in 1859, the *Venetian* was listed (and is still listed) as vessel No 1 in Harland & Wolff's order book. Gustav Wolff became Harland's partner in 1860, the year that the *Sicilian* and *Syrian* (Nos 2 and 3 in the order book) were launched, and in 1861 the company officially changed its name to become Harland & Wolff.

Harland married Rosa Wann of Vermont, Belfast, in 1860. He

Above: Although his father was an Ulsterman, William Pirrie was born in Canada, like the shipping magnate Samuel Cunard. He was brought to County Down as a baby and started work at Harland & Wolff as a premium apprentice when he was just 15. He succeeded Sir Edward Harland as chairman of the company 33 years later.

highly qualified professional such as an engineer.

William James Pirrie was born in Quebec, Canada, in 1847. His father, an Ulsterman, died when his son was still only a baby and his mother, Eliza, took William home to County Down where he spent his childhood in Conlig near Bangor. As a boy he went to primary school in Belfast before attending the Belfast Royal Academical Institute. From there he went to Harland & Wolff, where as a premium apprentice he was treated as a management trainee, moving from department to department but working principally as a draughtsman. By 1869 he was held in such high regard by the senior management at the yard that he was appointed chief designer on the yard's prestigious new vessel, the *Oceanic*. In 1874, at the age of just 27, Pirrie was made a partner at Harland & Wolff. His boundless energy and enthusiasm saw him at the yard, where he involved himself in all aspects of the business, from early in the morning until late into the evening. Ambitious and forceful, Pirrie was determined to manoeuvre himself into positions of ever greater authority at the shipyard. He genuinely enjoyed being involved in all aspects of the business, revelling in the excitement of working on state-of-the-art vessels, ships that incorporated all of the latest, most modern technological developments; ships that were bigger, better and faster than ever before.

In 1879 Pirrie married Margaret Montgomery Carlisle, the sister of one of Harland & Wolff's foremost designers, Alexander Carlisle. When Pirrie took over from Sir Edward Harland as chairman of Harland & Wolff, the Pirries also bought Ormiston House, a large, imposing mansion in East Belfast where Harland had lived until his death on Christmas Eve 1895. The house had always had shipping connections. Originally built in Glasgow, it was imported to Ulster stone-by-stone by Coombe Reid, a wealthy Scot involved in Belfast's shipbuilding industry. Ormiston was surrounded by extensive garden grounds with views down to Queen's Island and the Harland & Wolff yards, and it was there in 1897 that Pirrie, by then Lord Mayor of Belfast, played host to the Duke and Duchess of York, inviting thousands of Sunday school children to meet his guests. As well as becoming Lord Mayor of Belfast, Pirrie also served on the Harbour Commission and was made a baron in 1906.

became chairman of the Harbour Commission and was also involved in politics, standing as Mayor of Belfast in 1885 and 1886, when he was created a baron. Three years later he was elected as the MP for the Northern Division of Belfast and was re-elected in 1892 and 1895. Like Sir Edward Harland, Gustav Wolff also became involved in politics and served as the MP for East Belfast from his election in 1892 until his retirement eight years later. He was chairman of the Belfast Ropework Company and had a house in Strandtown, Belfast, although in the latter part of his life he spent less and less time in Ulster and died in London in 1913. Sir Edward Harland remained closely involved with Harland & Wolff up to his death in 1895. The role of chairman of the company was taken by William James Pirrie.

Pirrie began his career at Harland & Wolff in 1862 at the age of 15, hired by a company that then had only around 100 employees as a premium or 'gentleman' apprentice. Such an apprenticeship had to be bought, the apprentice, or rather the apprentice's parents paying up to £100 to secure the position for their son. This made the premium apprenticeship attainable only by well-educated, middle-class boys, as the price represented more than a year's wages for a skilled working class tradesman and around three months' salary even for a

Part of the *Stirling Castle*'s rudder stock is hoisted into place in 1935 from the flat bed of a Harkness & Co. wagon. Harkness were local hauliers who had transported much of the heavy equipment for installation on the *Titanic*.

Lord and Lady Pirrie enjoyed the comfort of Downshire House when they were in London, but they also owned Witley Park, an extensive estate in Surrey. The house and grounds at Witley Park were bought by Lord Pirrie following the death of the man who had created the estate, the disgraced financier Whitaker Wright, who took cyanide after receiving a prison sentence when his business empire collapsed. Wright had acquired Witley Park in 1890, spending the remarkable sum of £840,000 to develop the mansion and a further £500,000 on the grounds. There were three lakes, below one of which he had constructed a ballroom with a glass roof. More money was spent in building the wall surrounding the 1,400 acres (567 hectares) of land than one of the bricklayers would earn in a lifetime. Lord Pirrie paid substantially less for the property than had been spent creating it.

Lord Pirrie, then, was a man of great wealth and influence by the time he and Joseph Bruce Ismay conceived of the Olympic-class liners. Ismay, too, although he was 15 years younger than the master shipbuilder, was a man of some substance. These were not two woolly-headed dreamers conjuring up some fanciful scheme to build the world's biggest ship. Both knew precisely what they were doing. Lord Pirrie had many years of experience in building world-renowned ships, and Ismay was in charge of the most powerful shipping organisation on the planet. The two also had a unique understanding that stemmed from the long-standing relationship between Harland & Wolff and the White Star Line.

Formed in 1845, the White Star Line had operated sailing ships to the Far East and Australia during the Australian gold rush, but when gold fever subsided so, too, did the fortunes of the White Star Line. The shipping company went into liquidation with debts of over £500,00 and was bought up by Thomas Ismay in 1868. Ismay, the son of a shipbuilder, had started his working life in the 1850s as an apprentice at the Liverpool shipbrokers Imrie, Tomlinson & Co, but had big plans to create a steamship company. In partnership with William Imrie, Ismay set up the Oceanic Steam Navigation Company, buying the White Star Line's name and flag for £1,000, a deal that was financed by the German entrepreneur Gustav Schwabe. Schwabe and

Ismay agreed that as part of the deal the new company's new ships would be built at the Belfast shipyard of Schwabe's nephew, Gustav Wolff. From then on, the futures of White Star and Harland & Wolff were forged together as White Star's new ships would be paid for partly in cash and partly in White Star Line shares. Harland & Wolff, therefore, came to own a large interest in the White Star Line over subsequent years.

The first ship ordered by White Star was the *Oceanic*, one of the first of a new breed of ocean liner. Built on a grand scale, *Oceanic* was not only large but also thoroughly modern. Harland & Wolff had designed the *Oceanic* differently from most previous ships, with the superstructure combined as part of the hull rather than simply bolted on to the deck. Other modern passenger conveniences, such as running water in all of her cabins, made the *Oceanic* truly remarkable, and these qualities of innovation and luxury were to become the proud hallmark of the White Star ships built by Harland & Wolff. By the time Thomas Ismay's eldest son, Joseph, joined his father's business, the White Star Line was thriving and had established an enviable reputation for the opulence of its passenger accommodation.

Joseph was certainly no stranger to the White Star fleet. Born in 1862, as a boy he was brought up in a house with a view out over the estuary where the River Mersey flows into the Irish Sea. The White Star ships were easy for young Joseph to spot – they were the ones that sounded their horns in salute as they passed his house! The family later moved to a mansion Thomas Ismay had built in the Wirral. Educated at Elstree School and Harrow, J Bruce Ismay, as he is usually known, worked for the White Star Line in New York where, during the 1880s, he cut quite a dash in society circles.

In 1888 he was married to Julia Florence Schieffelin in New York, a wedding that no one in high society would have wanted to miss. The ceremony was held at the Church of the Heavenly Rest on Fifth Avenue. The bride was resplendent in a gown of white brocade trimmed with old point lace, her lace veil was held in place by a diamond tiara and a diamond pendant hung from a perfect string of pearls around her neck. After the ceremony the reception was held at the bride's parents'

Far left: Joseph Bruce Ismay succeeded his father, Thomas, as chairman of the White Star Line in 1899 at the age of 37. He presided over the sale of White Star to the IMMC and, five years after the takeover, J Bruce Ismay was chairman the IMMC and one of the most powerful shipping magnates in the world.

Left: Thomas Andrews joined Harland & Wolff as a premium apprentice in 1889. By the time the *Titanic* was taking shape in 1910, Andrews was in charge of Harland & Wolff's design department.

residence on East Forty-Ninth Street and the newly-weds seemed destined to enjoy a privileged and affluent New York lifestyle. Their first daughter, Florence, was born in 1889 and she was followed by a son, Henry. Sadly, Henry fared badly during a stiflingly hot summer in New York in 1891, suffering chronic diarrhoea and other ailments that prompted the Ismays' doctor to advise that he be taken away from the overheating city, with an ocean voyage hopefully helping to restore his health. The young family travelled to Liverpool on the *Teutonic*, but little Henry's condition grew worse and he died shortly after arriving in England.

The Ismays settled in Liverpool in a mansion called Sandheys at Mossley Hill, from where J Bruce would walk the four miles (six kilometres) to the White Star offices in Water Street. In 1896 the company moved into a brand-new building nearby on the corner of James Street and the Strand designed by the architect R N Shaw, who had also been responsible for Scotland Yard's new headquarters in London. On 23 November 1899, Thomas Ismay died at his mansion, Dawpool, and was buried at the nearby Thurstaston cemetery. J Bruce Ismay succeeded his father as chairman of the White Star Line, and within a year was in negotiations with J P Morgan for the sale of the company. This is not to suggest that Thomas Ismay's beloved White Star Line was sold on almost as soon as he was gone – the sale was more a matter of remaining competitive in a very competitive market. Ismay, along with Lord Pirrie who was a

major White Star shareholder in his own right as well as on behalf of Harland & Wolff, negotiated a huge sum for the takeover of the company by J P Morgan's IMMC, but Ismay also secured the promise of a powerful new appointment. Two years after the takeover went through in 1904, J Bruce Ismay took over from American Line president A C Griscom as chairman of the IMMC. He was now in control of the most powerful commercial shipping operation in the world.

While J Bruce Ismay was responsible for running the IMMC, the finance behind the organisation came from the legendary J P Morgan. John Pierpont Morgan was a man of truly formidable stature. He had been a powerful force in the American economy for over 30 years at a time when the American economy was fast becoming a barometer for industrial, commercial and financial change the world over. Decisions made by Morgan reached out from his Wall Street offices to touch the lives of ordinary people not only in America, but also pretty much everywhere else on the planet. He was involved in the evolving railroad business in America and in 1892 was behind the merger that created the giant General Electric company. He was one of a select few financiers who saved the US government from bankruptcy in 1895 (for a tidy profit) and he bought out Andrew Carnegie to create US Steel in 1901. Morgan also bought up collapsing US mining operations to rescue Wall Street from a similar collapse in 1907. Around this time his personal fortune was estimated to be around $20 billion – a vast sum, but Morgan had always been used to having or being around money.

J P Morgan was born in 1837 in Hartford, Connecticut, the son of a wealthy banker. He went to university in Gottingen, Germany, and by 1857 he was working on Wall Street, establishing his own investment company in 1861 and taking over his father's banking business when his father passed away in 1890. While he was known as a great philanthropist, establishing among other public institutions the Morgan Library in New York and assembling the largest-ever private collection of works of art, much of which is now on display at New York's Metropolitan Museum, Morgan's reputation as a businessman was ferocious. Used to getting his own way and ruthless in pursuit of his ambitions, Morgan demanded respect even from the president of the United States and what he demanded was usually exactly what he got. In order to further his desire for a North Atlantic shipping monopoly, in 1907 he is said to have demanded of J Bruce Ismay that he should 'get me the finest vessels afloat'. Ismay would have needed no second bidding – this was his chance to place his beloved White Star Line so far ahead of the competition that it would take his rivals ten years to catch up.

The sketches for the new Olympic-class liners that Lord Pirrie handed to his design team became the responsibility of his brother-in-law, Alexander M Carlisle, who was chairman of the managing directors of Harland & Wolff and ultimate head of the design department. Having started at Harland & Wolff as an apprentice, Carlisle had worked at the yard for 37 years by the time work began on the Olympic-class ships. Although Carlisle was in overall charge of the ships' drawings and the draughtsmen, he always maintained that the Olympic-class vessels were actually designed almost entirely by Lord Pirrie. Refining Lord Pirrie's designs, however, into the thousands of incredibly detailed engineering drawings required for the construction of a ship was the task that fell to Carlisle and the managing director of the design department, Thomas Andrews, who was also Lord Pirrie's nephew.

Andrews came from one of Ulster's most highly respected families. They had a number of business interests, including in the linen industry. Thomas Andrews' father (also called Thomas) was a distinguished local politician, his uncle was a high court judge and his brother became Prime Minister of Northern Ireland. Born in February 1873, Thomas was educated at the Royal Belfast Academical Institute, just as both his father and Lord Pirrie had been. Again like Pirrie, Thomas joined Harland & Wolff as a premium apprentice and he threw himself into studying every aspect of the shipbuilding business. He learned the trades of the skilled workers who built the ships and attended evening classes in technical drawing, mechanics, engineering and naval architecture. On finishing his apprenticeship, Thomas worked as a manager in the repair yard and in 1901, 12 years after joining Harland & Wolff, his professional skills and qualifications were recognised when he became a member of the prestigious Institute of Naval Architects.

Around this time he was also appointed manager of Harland & Wolff's construction works. He was involved in the building of the White Star liners the *Adriatic*, *Baltic*, *Cedric* and *Celtic* as well as ships for the Holland-America and Red Star lines, and those who worked with him found him to be conscientious, charming and good-natured. While his colleagues might well have thought it advantageous to speak well of Thomas Andrews – he was, after all Lord Pirrie's nephew (the son of Pirrie's sister, Eliza) – the regard and affection in which he was held seems to have been entirely genuine. Their faith in him would ultimately be borne out by the strength of character he displayed during subsequent events aboard the *Titanic*.

In June 1908, with work on the final designs for the Olympic-class ships nearing completion, Thomas Andrews married Helen Reilly Barbour, the daughter of a former director of Harland & Wolff, and two years later their only child, Elizabeth, was born. The year 1910 also marked the retirement from Harland & Wolff of Lord Pirrie's brother-in-law, Alexander Carlisle. Carlisle has variously been described as a close confidant of Pirrie, a free thinker who could not stand the autocratic manner in which Pirrie chose to run Harland & Wolff and an eccentric and hugely talented ship designer. His direct area of responsibility on the Olympic-class ships had been the design and specification of

Above: Although certain specialised castings were supplied by outside companies, such as the Darlington Forge Company which provided the brackets that housed the propeller shafts, the rudder and its mounting, Harland & Wolff also operated its own foundry. Note the foreman or overseer who wears a bowler hat while the other men wear flat caps. Foremen at the yard were known as 'hats'.

their equipment and, in conjunction with Thomas Andrews, he had recommended that there be three lifeboats at each davit, a total of 48 boats, although 64 boats were proposed at one time. This number was gradually reduced during discussions with Lord Pirrie and J Bruce Ismay until there were only 16 standard 30-foot (9-metre) boats plus four collapsibles. The debate rages even now about whether the provision of more lifeboats on the *Titanic* would actually have helped to save more lives given that they barely had time to launch the few they did have. But arguing points such as this – and losing – may well have contributed to Carlisle's decision to retire when he reached 40 years' service with the company. His position was filled by Thomas Andrews.

All of the aforementioned men, from William Ritchie way back in the eighteenth century right up to Thomas Andrews, played a part in the building of the *Titanic*. For some, such as Gustav Schwabe (who died in 1890 and so knew nothing of the Olympic-class liners) or J P Morgan, supplying the finances and dabbling in shipping was an interesting, entertaining, even glamorous way of increasing their personal fortunes. For others, such as Lord Pirrie, J Bruce Ismay or Thomas Andrews, the White Star Line ships were a major part of their lives. They spent every day discussing, developing and planning the finest ocean liners in the world and they knew every plate, every bulkhead, every rivet of the ships as they were being built. But even they did not have the very real, honest, physical connection

with the *Titanic* of the men who really built her, the men of Belfast who worked in the Harland & Wolff yard.

The men who worked in the shipyards, their families and the people of Belfast were immensely proud of the ships that had been built on the River Lagan. They regarded Belfast-built ships as the best constructed in the world and, to the credit of the Belfast workers, the rest of the world tended to agree with them. The great pride taken by the people of Belfast in the city's ships grew from the way that the ships dominated the lives of so many. In the shipyards the dormant steel giants grew from nothing into massive shapes that could be seen and admired from a distance by anyone who cared to walk to the end of their street or crane their necks while standing on their own doorsteps. The noise of the hammering of rivets was a constant reminder that another Belfast ship was taking shape, the sight and sound of its creation making it very much a part of the everyday life of everyone in the city.

The people most affected by the new vessels were the workers who lived with the *Titanic* and her sister ships throughout their construction every working day from 6.00 in the morning until 5.30 at night. They ate, not in the company dining rooms enjoyed by the shipyard's management, but in the shadow of the ships themselves, bringing their own food for a brief breakfast break at **8.30** am and another short break for lunch at 1.00 pm. They worked up to 60 hours a week, including Saturday mornings, and would suffer stoppages from their pay if they were late for work – whatever the reason – damaged company tools or equipment, or transgressed any of the shipyards rules and regulations. Even if workers went to watch the launch of a vessel on which they had worked, they could expect to lose a day's pay. Shipyard workers could look forward to one week's holiday in the summer, with two days off for both Christmas and Easter, all for an average wage that amounted to around £2 per week.

Senior staff or managers at the yard had things a little easier, but if they were responsible for other staff or had men reporting to them, they had to be at their posts *before* 6.00 am to supervise the arrival of the workforce. Lord Pirrie, naturally, was the exception. It was his habit while in Belfast to arrive at the

The Harland & Wolff shipyard in the early 1900s before it came to be dominated by the massive steel latticework of the Arrol Gantry below which the Olympic-class liners would take shape.

yard at 7.00 am and spend much of the day checking on the progress being made in every department. Unlike the workforce, he was not expected to clock in and clock out. The Harland & Wolff workforce, 15,000 men at the time the *Titanic* was being built, left their Belfast terraced houses before it was light (except for a few brief weeks during the summer months when dawn came early) and swarmed around the shipyard's entrance. There they were joined by crowds of casual labourers hoping to be taken on for the day at one of the regular early-morning hiring sessions if one of the shipyard's foremen needed a few extra pairs of hands.

For many, securing regular employment at the yard meant following in their father's footsteps and learning a trade. Apprentices could be taken on as young as 14, with most apprenticeships lasting five years. The trades they could learn were many and varied. Harland & Wolff handled every aspect of a ship's construction from the laying of the keel, the framing and plating, through to the building of the engines, the installation of the equipment and fittings and the interior décor. In common with other manufacturing industries and general trades, an apprentice was expected to supply the basic tools of his trade, traditionally paid for – at least in part – by his journeyman, the qualified tradesman to whom he was apprenticed. After serving for five years, an apprentice could look forward to carrying a union card that identified him as a qualified plumber, coppersmith, riveter, plater, joiner, driller, craneman, decorator, blacksmith, ironworker, woodturner, fitter, shipwright, caulker, electrician, painter or any one of a dozen other trades.

While it was a good thing to have a safe and secure job, a shipyard was by no means a safe and secure place to work. Industrial accidents in the nineteenth and early twentieth centuries were an occupational hazard and fatalities were commonplace. In the shipbuilding industry there was a rule of thumb that it was acceptable to incur one death among the workforce for every £100,000 spent on a project. Building the *Titanic* was to cost £1.5 million. When construction was completed, a report was submitted to a Harland & Wolff management meeting listing the casualties incurred during work on the *Titanic*. There were 254 recorded accidents: 69 in the

engine works, of which 6 were listed as 'severe', and 185 in the shipyard, 8 of which were fatalities. The total amount of compensation payments for the 254 accidents was £4,849 3s 5d. The company even bought two new motor cars to be used as ambulances, kept ready near the main gate to take injured workers to hospital as quickly as possible. When work finished for the day, or at weekends when the shipyard was closed, the cars were hired out to help pay for their upkeep. Scandalous though it may seem today, eight deaths on such a huge project was well within the 'acceptable' industry norm at that time. Because it has become such a legend, it is easy to forget that the *Titanic* was built almost a century ago when health and safety standards throughout the industrial world were simply not comparable with those of today – if, indeed, they existed at all. Harland & Wolff's safety standards were no worse than in any other shipyard, not that this detracts in any way from the tragedy for the families and friends of the eight workers who died.

Of those eight fatalities, two were from riveting squads. This should come as no surprise considering how dangerous the riveters' job could be. Riveters worked on every part of the ship, from the dimly-lit enclosed spaces inside the hull to breezy platforms over 80 feet (24 metres) high on the scaffolding or staging surrounding the ship. The *Titanic's* entire steel structure was held together by simple rivets rather than welded joints, as welding at that time was still in its infancy. This made the riveting squads the kings of the shipyard, who earned respect from the other tradesmen for their skill and courage because, as if the circumstances of their work were not dangerous enough, the job itself was not without its hazards.

A riveting squad normally consisted of four or five men: the heater boy, the catch boy, the holder-on (in some cases the catch boy might double as a holder-on) and two riveters. The heater boy's job was to tend a coke-fired brazier or furnace in which the individual rivets were heated. He knew that, when the rivet turned a certain colour, he had to lift it out of the fire and get it to the riveters as quickly as possible. Plucking the rivet out of the furnace using tongs, he then rolled it down a chute to the catch boy who would pick it up using his own tongs and run with it to where the riveters were working. There he would hand

Above: A work party stands by a bed of sand in the foundry. Iron or steel items were made by pouring molten metal into moulds carved in the sand where the metal cooled and took on the desired basic shape. This basic casting method is still in use today.

it on to the holder-on who would seat the rivet in the hole drilled through the two overlapping steel plates and the riveters – one left-handed and one right handed – would begin hammering on either side of the plates.

The riveters swung their 4-pound (1.8-kilogram) hammers in unison, striking both ends of the rivet at exactly the same instant to pound the red-hot rivet heads into the desired shape, squeezing the steel plates together. If they mistimed their initial strikes, the riveter whose hammer hit first could send a red-hot rivet shooting out of the opposite side of the plates – an extremely dangerous and costly error. The riveters, however, were masters of their craft and the ringing of the double strikes of their hammers could be heard for miles around. After a time, the noise would make them deaf. Just like a blacksmith working at a forge, the riveters would lose a lot of sweat and generally kept a good supply of drinking water nearby to stop them from dehydrating during the course of the day.

The men had to work fast to make sure the rivet was in place while it was still hot enough to be worked, but there was another good reason for their frenetic pace – they were paid by the rivet. A tally was kept of the number of rivets seated by each squad and at the end of the week the squad would be paid

accordingly. The workers were then left to divide the money among themselves as they saw fit. This meant that everyone in the team wanted to be seen to be pulling their weight and the heater boys and catch boys were under constant pressure to keep the riveters supplied. Rushing to retrieve or deliver the next red-hot rivet was often the cause of accidents. One of the two riveting squad fatalities during the construction of the *Titanic* was 15-year-old catch boy, Samuel Scott; the other was 19-year-old heater boy John Kelly. One fell from a ladder on the staging, the other fell from the slipway.

Even as the *Titanic* was launched, with the assembled dignitaries and shipyard employees cheering as she entered the water for the first time, a tragedy was being played out on the slipway. Shipwright James Dobbin had been knocking away shoring beams beneath the hull immediately prior to the launch when some of the timbers collapsed on top of him. He was seriously injured and his workmates dragged him clear of the slipway and rushed him to hospital where he later died from his injuries. Sadly, James Dobbin would not be the last of the Belfast workforce to lose his life to the *Titanic*.

When a ship left the Harland & Wolff yard, completed its sea trials and was properly certified by the Board of Trade as being fit and ready to receive passengers, it was officially handed over to its owners to set sail on its maiden voyage. The ship's crew, her engineers and officers are not, at this point, as familiar with the ship as the men who built her, so it was normal practice for the shipyard to send a team of key personnel with the ship as advisors or to help deal with any teething problems. At Harland & Wolff this team was known as the guarantee group. Only the best, most proficient, most highly regarded of the shipyard workers who had built the ship could expect to be selected as part of the guarantee group. Those who were selected knew that their foremen, their managers and the company hierarchy valued their skills, trusting them to acquit themselves well, represent the company in a professional, efficient manner, and conduct themselves with dignity and pride. They also knew that having been recognised as a key employee, their future with the company was assured. For all of these reasons, it was considered a great honour to be selected as part of a guarantee group.

Just over half of Harland & Wolff's workforce was required for the building of the *Olympic* and *Titanic*. Work in other parts of the complex continued, where they manufactured not only machinery and parts for their own ships, but also items to order. This boiler is being loaded onto a ship for export in 1910.

The majority of those in Harland & Wolff's guarantee groups would have been incredibly excited about this wonderful opportunity. They were, after all, being rewarded for their exemplary work with a trip on an ocean liner. For many this was the first time they had ever been on a ship that was actually doing what it was designed and built to do – sail across the ocean. This was a chance to see how well the fixtures and fittings they had installed actually performed, or to learn how easy or difficult it was to operate the equipment while the ship was at sea. Practical problems that might evolve during the everyday use of a winch, a pulley or pumping equipment, the siting of a hatch, the run of a pipe or the opening of a door could be corrected or borne in mind for future reference.

The leader of the guarantee group that sailed with the *Titanic* in 1912 was, almost inevitably, Thomas Andrews. He knew every plate, beam, passage, boiler and bulkhead on the *Titanic* better than anyone else and he was ideally placed to represent Harland & Wolff at the highest level. It was expected that when Lord Pirrie ultimately retired, Thomas Andrews would be the man to take over the company. Andrews made copious notes while aboard the *Titanic*. He carried a notebook with him in which he would jot down any ideas that came to him for improvements or refinements that might be made to the *Titanic* design when it came to building the *Gigantic*, the third of the Olympic-class liners.

Accompanying Andrews was Roderick Chisholm. A Scotsman born in Dumbarton in 1872, Chisholm had been working at Harland & Wolff in Belfast since 1892. He and his wife, Susan, had been married for 16 years and had two children, 15-year-old Alyce and 14-year-old Jimmy. Chisholm had risen to the position of chief draughtsman and had worked closely with Andrews on the designs of both the *Olympic* and *Titanic*. He had actually designed the *Titanic's* lifeboats, although the number of lifeboats carried on the ship was not his decision.

Not far from the Chisholms' home lived another senior member of the guarantee group. Anthony Frost, Artie to those who knew him well, was a 38-year-old foreman fitter who, unlike many of his contemporaries, had spent a great deal of time aboard ships at sea. He had finished his Harland & Wolff apprenticeship as a fitter in 1894 and then left the yard to spend two years at sea. Five years after he returned to the Belfast yard, Frost was promoted to leading hand fitter and in 1907, when his father, a foreman fitter, retired, Frost was given his job. Married to Lizzie Jane, the couple had four children.

Former railwayman William Parr was an assistant manager in the electrical department at Harland & Wolff, in charge of overseeing the wiring and electrical fittings on both the *Olympic* and *Titanic*. Born in Lancashire in 1882, Parr had worked as an electrician on the Lancashire and Yorkshire Railway before joining Harland & Wolff in 1910. Married with a young child, Parr was a much-respected Sunday school teacher. Parr had a promising career ahead of him at Harland & Wolff, as did Robert Knight who had worked at the yard for 21 years. Married with four children, Knight was a leading hand fitter and a conscientious worker whom most expected to be promoted to foreman before long.

Another hard worker was 18-year-old Ennis Hastings Watson. Watson was an apprentice electrician who had been studying art, electrical wiring and fitting at the Belfast Municipal Technical Institute since 1907. No one doubted that he would soon become a fully-qualified electrician, especially his proud parents with whom he still lived.

Francis Parks also lived with his parents in Belfast, having been brought up in the city along with his four brothers and two sisters. Although their father was employed not at the shipyard but as an official with Belfast City Council, all five brothers worked for Harland & Wolff. Parks was an apprentice plumber when he was selected to join the *Titanic's* guarantee group and would have had much in common with another apprentice, Alfred Cunningham. Cunningham had two sisters, and three brothers. As an apprentice fitter, he worked on the guarantee group under the watchful eye of his foreman, Mr Frost. The final member of the nine-man guarantee group was another teenaged apprentice, William Campbell, an apprentice joiner who lived with his parents in Belfast.

None of the Harland & Wolff guarantee group was to survive the sinking of the *Titanic*.

Titanic's first-class reading room was situated on the port side of A deck, the second-highest level of the ship. The white-painted wood panelling reflected the light that streamed in through the massive bay window that looked out over the promenade.

GRAND DESIGNS

Turning the concepts sketched out by Lord Pirrie and J Bruce Ismay in Belgrave Square into engineering drawings from which a ship could be built was an exacting and time-consuming process, not least because the detail of the designs changed many times. The three new Olympic-class ships were visualised by Lord Pirrie and J Bruce Ismay as being virtually identical, but it quickly became clear that, for entirely practical reasons, only two could be built initially, with the third to follow at a later date. Attempting to build the world's three largest ships simultaneously at Harland & Wolff's yard would have been almost an impossibility.

The *Olympic* and *Titanic* were to be produced first. They were designed using almost identical drawings and general plans, although changes during the design and construction meant that some relatively minor differences developed between the *Olympic* and *Titanic*. Nevertheless, they were still very much recognisable as sister ships. Pirrie and Ismay originally envisaged them as being around 100 feet (30 metres) longer than the Cunard liners *Lusitania* and *Mauretania*. They saw their new ships as having four masts and three funnels but soon revised this to two masts and four funnels. The popular conception was that the number of funnels equated directly to the power and majesty of the vessel; since the *Lusitania* and *Mauretania* had four funnels, then the Olympic-class ships also had to have four. For all practical purposes, however, venting the smoke from the *Olympic* or *Titanic's* boilers would require only three funnels, the fourth funnel being little more than a show piece only used for ventilation. From the tops of these funnels, which stood over 60 feet (18 metres) above the boat deck, down through the ship's superstructure to the bottom of the keel would be a towering 175 feet (53 metres).

Once the funnel issue was resolved, attention could be focused on the hull dimensions. Constructing a ship 100 feet (30 metres) longer than the Cunarders was a daunting undertaking. The Tyne-built *Mauretania* outstretched her Clyde-built sister ship to achieve a length of about 790 feet (240 metres). The plans drawn up for the *Olympic* and *Titanic* showed them each to be 882 feet 9 inches (269 metres) in

length, although in many specification lists the *Olympic's* length is often rounded up to 883 feet (269.1 metres). The *Titanic* was actually undersized when advertised on White Star Line posters as being 882 feet 6 inches (268.9 metres) and, further to add to the confusion, the *Titanic* is regularly quoted as being 4 inches (10 centimetres) longer than the *Olympic*.

Arguments over those few inches will doubtless continue to wash back and forth forever, but the fact remains that, when she entered service, the *Olympic* fulfilled the dream of Lord Pirrie and J Bruce Ismay. She was the largest ship in the world and was to remain so until the *Titanic* was handed over by Harland & Wolff to the White Star Line. The *Olympic's* gross tonnage was 45,324, the *Titanic's* 46,428, making the *Titanic* indisputably the world's largest ship at that time. Design details made all the difference to the *Titanic's* tonnage, but the general look of the ships was still the same – these were, after all, the 'Olympic-class' sister ships. Here, of course, it makes most sense to concentrate on the design and layout of the *Titanic*.

The plans drawn up for the *Titanic* showed nine decks, ten if the lowest platform known as the Tank Top, was included. For ease of identification by future passengers, the seven decks where there would be passenger accommodation were referred to by letters of the alphabet, from the second highest deck, the Promenade Deck (A), to the Lower Deck (G). Above the Promenade Deck was the Boat Deck and below the Lower Deck (it wasn't actually the lowest) were the Orlop Deck and then the Tank Top.

The Tank Top was the real basement of the ship. Moving aft, the cargo holds and reserve coal holds at the bow gave way to No 6 boiler room, which housed four of the ship's 29 enormous boilers. Each of these boilers was like a gigantic drum, 15 feet 9 inches (5 metres) in diameter with three furnaces at either end (they were known as 'double-ended' boilers), heating the water in the boiler to provide steam for the engines. At either end of No 6 boiler room were its cavernous coal bunkers, built as closely as possible to the furnaces to make the back-breaking job of shovelling coal into the hungry furnaces a little easier. Not that this arrangement was made out of compassion for the wellbeing of the stokers – speed and efficiency in stoking the furnaces was of primary importance.

Aft of No 6 boiler room was, unsurprisingly, No 5 boiler room. The ship's hull at this point was reaching its widest, the width (or beam) of the *Titanic* a mighty 92 feet 6 inches (28.2 metres). This was over 4 feet (1.2 metres) wider than the *Mauretania*. Having more width with which to play, No 5 boiler room could take an extra boiler and five were fitted here side by side, with the coal bunkers to feed their furnaces fore and aft of the boilers just as in boiler room No 6. The smoke from the furnaces of boiler rooms 6 and 5 was carried up through chimney flues that passed through every other deck of the ship to disperse via the foremost funnel.

Boiler rooms No 4 and No 3 were laid out in a similar fashion to No 5 with five boilers and the smoke from their furnaces venting through the second funnel, while boiler rooms No 2 and No 1 fed their furnace smoke out through the third fully functioning funnel. Boiler room No 1 was a little different in that the five boilers it housed were slightly smaller at 11 feet 9 inches (3.5 metres) long and had furnaces at only one end. These 'single-ended' boilers were used to provide steam for the machinery while the *Titanic* was in port, where full power was not needed for the engines. Auxiliary steam pipes from other boiler rooms could also be used to power ancillary equipment such as steam-powered winches or electrical generators. The *Titanic* had a great many electrical fittings throughout the ship, burning many times more electricity than the largest, most modern hotels of the day.

Aft of boiler room No 1 was the main engine room, the largest space on the entire ship. The engine room soared up through the Orlop Deck, Lower Deck (G), Middle Deck (F) and Upper Deck (E), leaving the tops of the boiler rooms two decks below. At 59 feet (18 metres) long, the main engine room needed all of its length and height to accommodate the massive bulk of the two huge reciprocating engines, each as big as a three-storey house. Further toward the stern was another engine room, this one occupied by a smaller, yet slightly more powerful, turbine engine.

Harland & Wolff may have lacked experience with turbines and may not have had all of the technological advantages that the builders of the Cunard turbine-powered liners enjoyed courtesy of their government funding, but they were following a tried-and-tested principle of evolution rather than revolution. The turbine that was installed did not provide the sole means of propulsion, the *Titanic* also had two huge 'piston' engines, but it was a modern innovation that ran very economically on the 'used' steam from the main engines. This steam otherwise would either have vented wastefully out of the funnels or have been cooled, condensed and fed back into the boilers to be reheated. While the turbine engine was not of the most advanced type, it certainly pulled, or rather pushed, its weight. In fact, it couldn't pull at all as it could only turn its central screw propeller in one direction, providing forward propulsion. The two more traditional engines each drove their own propeller, one on the left and one on the right side of the central screw.

Beyond the turbine room was a space housing the *Titanic's* four huge electrical generators, again producing power from steam. These were flanked by a series of fresh water storage tanks and aft of this compartment was the tapering stern of the ship where the drive shafts exited to the three gigantic propellers.

Above the Tank Top was the Orlop Deck and at the bow was a part-deck called the Lower Orlop Deck. In the *Titanic's* bows, the Orlop and Lower Orlop were used for general storage and the chain locker, the space where the anchor chain was stowed when the anchors were not in use. The chain locker extended all the way up through to F Deck. Then, as far back as No 6 boiler room, there were the forward cargo holds. It was here that the Renault car bought in France by the wealthy Philadelphian Billy Carter would be stored along with other items being shipped to the United States, such as the case of machinery for the Aero Club of America or the 856 rolls of linoleum being carried for McGrachlin & Co.

The Orlop Deck forward of No 6 boiler room was also earmarked to be used as a store for baggage belonging to first- and second-class passengers. The baggage store was on the port side of the ship while opposite, on the starboard side, was an equally large space devoted to the storage of the mail

Fig. 8.
LOWER DECK

Fig. 9. ORLOP DECK.

Fig. 10. TANK TOP.

These diagrams show the three lowest decks of the ship, the Tank Top, the Orlop Deck and the Lower Deck and ably demonstrate how the engine rooms and boiler rooms reached up from the floor of the ship at the Tank Top right into the heart of the vessel. These were the largest enclosed spaces on board and their towering size is often compared to that of a cathedral.

Fig. 11. LOWER ORLOP DECK

Below: Although difficult to decipher as it is split so as to look both forward and aft, this diagram shows how tightly the five boilers fitted into the belly of the ship and how the smoke they generated was fed via flues to the funnel.

BOAT DECK.

BOILER ROOM Nº 1
LOOKING AFT. 24 FRAME

PROMENADE DECK.

BRIDGE DECK.

STATE ROOMS   STATE ROOMS

SHELTER DECK.

1ST CLASS PANTRY   1ST CLASS PANTRY

SALOON DECK

PASSAGE

STATE ROOMS   BOILER ROOM Nº 2
                                     LOOKING FORWARD. 8 FRAME

UPPER DECK.

                                               3RD CLASS DINING SALOON

PASSAGE

MIDDLE DECK.

COAL   COAL

LOWER DECK.

Below: This plan of Boiler Rooms 1 & 2 shows the
single-ended boilers in No 1 and the double-ended
boilers in No 2 with their flues feeding up towards the
smoke stack or funnel.

PLAN OF BOILER ROOMS Nᵒˢ I AND 2

Fig. 4. SHELTER DECK. (C)

Fig. 5. SALOON DECK (D)

Fig. 6. UPPER DECK (E)

Fig. 7. MIDDLE DECK (F)

These plans of decks F to C show that, while passenger accommodation stretched all the way down to G Deck the first class cabins did not begin until E Deck. Facilities for first-class passengers, of course, extended into the lower decks with the swimming bath and steam room on F Deck and the floor of the squash court all the way down on G Deck.

Fig.2. PROMENADE DECK (A)

Fig.3.

POOP DECK.

BRIDGE DECK (B)

THE WHITE STAR LINERS
CONSTRUCTED BY MESSRS. HARLAND AND WOLFF,

Fig.12. BOAT DECK.

The plans of the three uppermost decks show how much space was allocated to the most expensive state rooms and to the first class public areas as well as how tragically few lifeboats were carried on the *Titanic*.

FIG. 12. THE

YMPIC" AND "TITANIC."

ED, SHIPBUILDERS AND ENGINEERS, BELFAST.

sacks, 3,364 of which would be carried on the *Titanic's* maiden voyage. Most of the rest of the length of the Orlop Deck, the vast belly of the ship, was taken up by boiler spaces, and engine and turbine rooms, but aft of the turbine, above the electrical generators, was another useful space. There was a switchboard platform where the electricity supply was routed to the various circuits around the ship and a number of storage spaces. A bulk store, steward's workstore and mineral water store were fitted in along with storerooms for groceries, fruit and vegetables, and wines and spirits. Next door to the wines and spirits store was a totally separate room solely for champagne, which some of the *Titanic's* first-class passengers would drink with every course during dinner. On the starboard side and to the rear of these storage areas were special refrigerator rooms for storing perishable cargo, with a further standard cargo hold right at the stern of the Orlop Deck.

Above the Orlop Deck on G Deck (Lower Deck) the bow space was used as a storage locker and the chain locker extended up from the deck below. Moving aft were the first of the *Titanic's* berths, a port dormitory where 15 leading firemen slept and a starboard one housing 30 greasers. Each of the dormitories had its own washroom and immediately aft of these crew quarters was the first passenger accommodation. Situated above the main forward cargo hold, was a large, full-width open dormitory for third-class passengers. Further first-class baggage holds separated these passenger berths from a smaller third-class dormitory area on the port side and the ship's post office on the starboard side. Directly above the mail storage area, and with its own secure storage for registered letters, 200 sacks of which were to travel with the *Titanic,* this was where the ship's five mail clerks would work, sorting the letters, parcels and packages while the ship was *en route* to New York.

Between the smaller port dormitory and the post office was the *Titanic's* squash court. This novel facility was 30 feet (9 metres) long, 20 feet (6 metres) wide and reached all the way up into F deck. Use of the squash court was restricted to first-class passengers. For those proficient enough to tackle a contest, the court could be booked at the enquiry office on C

Deck, at a cost of two shillings per half hour. For those who required a few pointers, a resident squash professional, Mr Frederick Wright, was on hand to provide tuition.

This forward area of G Deck then gave way to the bunkers, boilers and engine spaces that now included the engineers' stores, paint stores and workshops. Further toward the stern, aft of the turbine room, a cluster of food storage spaces for everything from beef, poultry, game and mutton to bacon, cheese, butter and ice cream held the bulk of the *Titanic's* extensive supply of provisions.

The aft section of G Deck housed the first of the passenger cabins – two or four-berth cabins for second-class passengers with one three-berther on both the port and starboard sides. These most basic second-class cabins were remarkably well appointed. Most had mahogany furniture, even though this consisted of upper and lower bunks, with curtains to provide a modicum of privacy for the occupants. They also had sofa beds that could be used as seating during the day, linoleum floor coverings rather than a bare, painted steel deck, electric lights, wood panelled walls and mahogany wash stands. The overall finish was to a standard that made the *Titanic's* second-class berths the equal of the majority of the White Star Line's rivals' first-class cabins. This second-class accommodation gave way to third-class two-, four- or 6-berth cabins at the ship's stern. The smallest, two-berth cabins had foldaway bunks to give more living space during the day but, even though these cabins provided the most spartan accommodation, they still had floor coverings, electric lights, and in most cases, a wash basin with running water. This was pure luxury compared with most other 'immigrant' ships of the period and a far better bedroom than many of the third-class passengers would have been used to at home!

Nevertheless, these cabins would be the least desirable on the ship as they were situated in one of the areas of the ship

that was likely to suffer most from pitching and swaying as she ploughed across the Atlantic. The bow and stern of a ship are subjected to more vertical movement as the vessel rides through the waves than the central section. The effect is rather like a see-saw, though not quite so extreme, with the ship 'pivoting' on the mid-section. The movement is generally felt most in the bow, where it is compounded by the crashing of waves, although in the stern lower decks passengers could also suffer from vibration caused by the propellers. That is why the lower-ranking crew members' quarters and the passengers who had bought the cheapest fares were housed in the bow or stern section accommodation.

The third-class cabins at the stern were also envisaged as being 'portable' because the walls could be moved to make them larger or smaller as required. Not only could the layout of the cabins be reconfigured, but the cabins could be stripped out altogether to convert the area into a cargo space. This was

Far left: This illustration is an artist's impression of a second-class cabin aboard the *Titanic*, produced for publicity purposes prior to the completion of the ship.

Left: The swimming bath was reserved for first-class passengers with ladies and gentlemen being allocated different periods during the day when they could swim. This photograph shows the *Olympic*'s pool, although it is identical to the one aboard the *Titanic*.

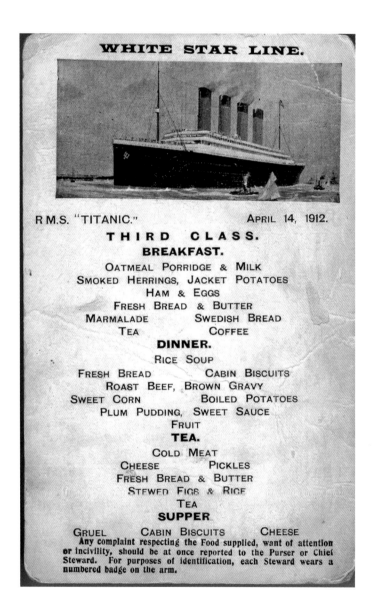

WHITE STAR LINE.

R.M.S. "TITANIC." APRIL 14, 1912.

THIRD CLASS.
BREAKFAST.
OATMEAL PORRIDGE & MILK
SMOKED HERRINGS, JACKET POTATOES
HAM & EGGS
FRESH BREAD & BUTTER
MARMALADE   SWEDISH BREAD
TEA   COFFEE
DINNER.
RICE SOUP
FRESH BREAD   CABIN BISCUITS
ROAST BEEF, BROWN GRAVY
SWEET CORN   BOILED POTATOES
PLUM PUDDING, SWEET SAUCE
FRUIT
TEA.
COLD MEAT
CHEESE   PICKLES
FRESH BREAD & BUTTER
STEWED FIGS & RICE
TEA
SUPPER
GRUEL   CABIN BISCUITS   CHEESE
Any complaint respecting the Food supplied, want of attention
or incivility, should be at once reported to the Purser or Chief
Steward. For purposes of identification, each Steward wears a
numbered badge on the arm.

R.M.S. "TITANIC."

APRIL 14, 1912.

LUNCHEON.
CONSOMMÉ FERMIER   COCKIE LEEKIE
FILLETS OF BRILL
EGG À L'ARGENTEUIL
CHICKEN À LA MARYLAND
CORNED BEEF, VEGETABLES, DUMPLINGS
FROM THE GRILL.
GRILLED MUTTON CHOPS
MASHED, FRIED & BAKED JACKET POTATOES

CUSTARD PUDDING
APPLE MERINGUE   PASTRY
BUFFET.
SALMON MAYONNAISE   POTTED SHRIMPS
NORWEGIAN ANCHOVIES   SOUSED HERRINGS
PLAIN & SMOKED SARDINES
ROAST BEEF
ROUND OF SPICED BEEF
VEAL & HAM PIE
VIRGINIA & CUMBERLAND HAM
BOLOGNA SAUSAGE   BRAWN
GALANTINE OF CHICKEN
CORNED OX TONGUE
LETTUCE   BEETROOT   TOMATOES
CHEESE.
CHESHIRE, STILTON, GORGONZOLA, EDAM,
CAMEMBERT, ROQUEFORT, ST. IVEL.
CHEDDAR

Iced draught Munich Lager Beer 3d. & 6d. a Tankard.

Above left: The third-class menu for all meals on 14 April 1912. The choices for the full day take up fewer lines than those for lunch alone in first class (right). For many third-class passengers, however, these could be the best meals they had ever eaten. For many, these would also be their last.

to make the return journey from New York to Southampton more profitable, as there were never likely to be as many passengers paying lower fares (mostly the 'immigrant trade') travelling eastbound across the Atlantic. There would always be some people, of course, who either found America not to be the land of opportunity of which they had dreamed, or who had made enough money to be able to return home to their families. These few thousand passengers each year, however, would not fill all of the berths on a ship such as the *Titanic* on every return trip. There was far more demand for goods produced or manufactured in the US to be transported back to Europe and these third-class cabins situated above the rear cargo hold could themselves be turned into a valuable cargo space.

Climbing up to F Deck, also known as the Middle Deck, the bow space was once more utilised in the traditional manner for storage with the chain locker immediately behind this space, and beyond that, following a familiar pattern, crew accommodation. These were to be the quarters of the ship's firemen and a handful of leading greasers. The forward section behind the crew facilities was taken up by over 70 third-class cabins, ranging in size from two to ten berths. Far more of the deck space could now be devoted to passenger accommodation as the intrusion from the boiler rooms below was greatly reduced, since the flues converged to be channelled upwards toward their allotted funnels. A larger intrusion from below was caused by the height of the squash court and its gallery for spectators.

On the starboard side of the squash court, surrounded by third-class cabins, were the mail clerks' berths, directly above the post office. Although space on the plans was allocated for only two clerks, the *Titanic* actually had five. These men were not employees of the White Star Line; they worked for the sea Post Office and were based in Southampton and New York. There had been some complaints from the postal workers on the *Olympic* about the siting of their berths as third-class passengers in the surrounding cabins kept them awake singing and partying into the small hours. The passengers could hardly be blamed – they were, after all, on a cruise bound for a new life in America and entitled to celebrate. The mail clerks,

however, had a full day's work ahead of them. During the voyage on the *Titanic*, this would mean sorting around 400,000 items of mail from the 1,758 sacks loaded at Southampton, 1,142 loaded at Cherbourg and 194 at Queenstown. They also had to deal with the postcards and letters mailed by the passengers while the ship was under way. Three of the mail clerks were American, William Gwinn, John March and Oscar Woody, while the others, John Smith and James Williamson, were British. On the evening of 14 April 1912, with the *Titanic* far out in the Atlantic, they were unlikely to be disturbed by the revelry of the passengers as they were celebrating Oscar Woody's forty-fourth birthday.

Moving aft from the passenger cabins, there were linen storage and drying rooms on the port side, while on the starboard side nestled one of the *Titanic's* most notable innovations – the swimming pool. The *Olympic* and *Titanic* were among the first ships ever to boast a swimming pool, but this was not the kind of makeshift, canvas-lined cargo hold some ships might call a swimming pool. The *Titanic's* swimming pool was indoor, bright and modern, flanked on one side by two shower stalls and a row of changing cubicles. On the other side daylight flooded in through an array of portholes. The pool, known as the swimming bath, was fully tiled and filled with heated salt water to a depth of 0 feet (1.0 metres). The final version on the finished ship was free for the use of male first-class passengers from 6.00am to 9.00am. Thereafter, tickets could be purchased from the enquiry office on C Deck for one dollar or four shillings. Ladies had exclusive use of the pool from 10.00am to 1.00pm and gentlemen could swim from 2.00pm to 6.00pm. Like the squash court, use of the swimming bath was restricted to first-class passengers whatever the time of day.

The swimming pool was not the only facility available on F Deck for the pampering of first-class passengers. Aft of the swimming bath were a separate steam room, hot room, temperate room, cooling room and shampoo room. This was the equivalent of what we would today call a leisure suite; on the *Titanic* it was called the Turkish bath. The Turkish bath operated on the same principle as the swimming bath with tickets available from the enquiry office, ladies from 10.00am until 1.00pm and gentlemen from 2.00pm until 6.00pm. The most incredible part of the Turkish bath was undoubtedly the cooling room, which was decorated in Arabian style. It was furnished with low loungers, canvas darkwood deck chairs and side tables where overheated refugees from the steam room or hot room could relax with a refreshing glass of cold water from the marble drinking fountain. Looking around, they could admire the intricate fretwork on what was described as 'an elaborately-carved Cairo curtain through which the light fitfully reveals something of the grandeur of the mysterious East'

In fact, the screens were disguising the rather less mysterious portholes through which light was fitfully emanating. The tiles covering the walls of this room above the teak dado rail were equally impressive. They were arranged in panels of blue and green, while on the ceiling the gilt-faced beams and cornices were complemented by bronze Arab lamps. The normal pillars, or stanchions, of the ship were suitably concealed behind carved teak casings, matching the teak panelling on the walls below the dado rail, and the floor was covered with a geometrically-patterned linoleum. If ever a first-class passenger wanted to forget that he or she was on board a ship, this was the place to do it.

Opposite the Turkish bath area on the port side beyond where the boiler room flues rose through the deck were storage rooms and dormitory berths for over 40 third-class stewards and 15 cooks. Aft of this section was the first of the passengers' public areas to stretch the full width of the ship, although again with the rising flues intruding. This was the third-class dining saloon, 100 feet (30 metres) long and formed by two rooms divided across the width of the ship by a bulkhead, but intended to be laid out uniformly. On the *Titanic* this would ultimately mean white enamel-painted walls and long tables laid for at least eight where the diners would eat breakfast, lunch (referred to as dinner in third class), dinner (called tea and served early evening) and a late supper.

The third-class passengers had their meals included in the price of their ticket but still ate handsomely. Breakfast might consist of porridge with milk, kippers or beefsteak and onions, jacket potatoes, fresh bread and butter, marmalade, tea or coffee. Dinner might start with soup followed by corned beef and cabbage with potatoes, then a fruit pudding such as peaches and rice. There would usually be a fish alternative to the meat course and kosher meat could be supplied for Jewish passengers. For tea there would be some kind of cooked course followed by cheese and pickles, then buns or bread and jam. Cheese, cabin biscuits, and tea or coffee were available at dinner or teatime, and also comprised the main elements of the late supper. This was a lot more food than many third-class passengers would ever have eaten before in one day. Up to 470 passengers could be served in the third-class dining saloon and there were three sittings for each meal.

Astern of the third-class dining saloon were the third-class pantries, the galleys and crew accommodation for butchers, bakers and stewards. Berths and facilities for the engineering crew filled the port and starboard sides of the next section of F Deck, separated by the higher part of the engine room. Beyond that, two- and four-berth second-class cabins were planned with two-, four-, five- and six-berth third-class cabins occupying the sternmost part of the deck. Although most cabins were intended to have some form of washing facility, there were no toilets in any of the cabins on either F or G Decks. In fact, there were no passenger toilet facilities planned for G Deck at all. Those in the stern cabins on G Deck would have to use the toilets located upstairs on F Deck, and those in the bow cabins on G and F Decks would have to make use of the facilities even further upstairs on E Deck.

In the very bow on E Deck, the Upper Deck, there was a store and crew dormitories for the ship's trimmers, who handled the coal for the furnaces. There were bunks for over 70 trimmers here as well as a further seamen's dormitory, crew facilities, washrooms and toilets for third-class passengers as well as a scattering of third-class cabins. Here, too, was the cabin of the master-at-arms, the man responsible for maintaining discipline aboard ship. The mid-section of the ship on the starboard side was devoted to crew's quarters from the carpenters and the quartermaster to the cooks, chefs, plate washers and bakers. Most of the accommodation here,

Right: Francis Browne was a 32-year-old student priest who travelled first class from Southampton aboard the *Titanic*, disembarking at Queenstown. He took many photographs during his short voyage including this one of the dressing table in his cabin.

however, was occupied by an army of waiters, stewards and assistant stewards. The passage outside their quarters was a constant bustle of to-ing and fro-ing as these crew members came on or off duty – so much so that this gangway became known as 'Scotland Road', named after a busy working-class area of Liverpool, the *Titanic's* home port.

The reason that all of these stewards and stewardesses were housed in the starboard mid-section of E Deck was because directly opposite, on the port side beyond the ever-decreasing intrusion of the boiler flues, were the first of the first-class cabins. For those first-class passengers who had not brought with them their own servants, it was imperative that their steward be readily available. Another, narrower, passageway ran past these first-class cabins. It was nicknamed 'Park Lane'.

These cabins were the most basic of the first-class accommodation. They were originally intended to sleep two, three or four, and had brass 'cot' beds with a low guard rail. This ran from the head part way down the side of the bed to stop those in a deep sleep rolling out of bed when the ship moved around in heavy seas. These guards, a common feature on ships' bunks, were also used on the beds in the more expensive first-class cabins, where they would become one of the few reminders that the room was actually a cabin aboard ship rather than a luxury hotel room. The E Deck cabins had wood panelling on the walls, concealing the ship's steel superstructure and pipework – the panelling was painted and hung with reproductions of works of art. The cabins were equipped with electric lighting and, of course, an electric bell-push to summon a steward at any time of the night or day. The passengers who would eventually occupy these cabins would pay £23 for their one-way ticket across the Atlantic. The ticket price did not include meals.

Aft of the first-class cabins on the starboard side were two- and four-berth second-class cabins and one larger cabin with berths allotted for five ship's musicians. In the end, more berths would have to have been found as the *Titanic* sailed with eight musicians. The violinist Wallace Hartley, who had been head-hunted from Cunard's *Mauretania*, was the band leader when the quartet played in the first-class dining room. The remaining trio, a violinist, cellist and pianist, would play alternately in the second-class dining room or the first-class reception room outside the *à la carte* restaurant on B Deck. Other crew members, such as the purser's clerks, were also allocated berths in second class on E Deck and space was also given over to the second-class barber's shop. There were two fully-equipped barber shops on board, one in second and one in first class, each boasting the most modern appliances – even hair dryers – and where gentlemen could enjoy a haircut or a luxurious shave seated in a proper barber's chair. The barber's

Left: A first-class suite, spacious enough easily to accommodate a table, couch and several chairs in the bedroom as well as the double bunk.

Above left: Another first-class suite in a different style, with the door open to show the private drawing room adjoining.

Above right: Yet another style of suite in first class, this time with a curtained four-poster-style double bunk.

shops also sold trinkets, souvenirs and postcards.

Opposite the second-class cabins, the starboard side of E deck comprised mainly of stores and crew quarters, while the after section was devoted to third-class cabins. Although it might seem strange to have sections of first-, second- and third-class cabins running concurrently on the same deck, the passengers were carefully segregated. It would not do to have those paying first-class fares mixing with those in third class, even though E Deck was the first deck where it was possible to walk all the way from the bow to the stern of the ship. To allow passengers to move between decks without straying into the wrong areas, there were separate third-, second- and first-class stairways. There were also separate elevators for first and second class (none for third). These were another of the *Titanic's* unique innovations, intended to give her even more of

the feel of a luxury hotel. Built and installed by the Otis elevator company, there were three elevators, each with an attendant, designed to be incorporated into the main first-class stairway and running from E Deck up to A (the Promenade) Deck. The single second-class elevator was built into the main second-class stairway in the after part of the mid-ship section and ran from F Deck all the way up to the Boat Deck. Like the three first-class elevators, there were stops on each deck.

Segregation was not only to be applied between the different classes of passenger, but also between the sexes in third class. Men and women travelling alone or unmarried were separated, the male berths in the bow third-class sections and the female in the stern sections. Obviously, it was expected that passengers travelling alone in first or second class would behave with the utmost of decorum, while it was thought best not to tempt the third-class travellers to turn the *Titanic* into *Love Boat*.

One area where the ladies and gentlemen travelling third class could mix freely was the third-class open space on D Deck, the Saloon Deck. Designed as a rather bland and spartan area behind the store and crew quarters in the bow of

Above left: This artist's impression, produced prior to the completion of the *Titanic*, shows passengers using two of the three first-class elevators.

Above right: Deck chairs and ornate décor in part of the *Titanic*'s Turkish baths complex.

D Deck, the open space was punctuated by the hatch that descended all the way down to the reserve coal bunkers on the Tank Top level and No 2 hatch, one of the ship's main cargo hatches. An obvious alternative use for the third-class open space was as an auxiliary cargo hold. Beyond this space, and distinctly separate from it, on both the port and starboard sides, were more first-class cabins with stewards' quarters tucked away here and there among the first-class washrooms. The passageways here led on to the first-class entrances on both the port and starboard sides. At the quayside or in the harbour when passengers were embarking, the doors through the hull into these halls would be the lowest level at which first-class passengers were able to board the ship. At sea the entrance halls were to form a link between the first-class cabin passageways and the first-class reception area.

In the reception area was the bottom of the magnificent grand staircase. The delicate, swirling wrought ironwork and intricate marquetary on the woodwork of the balustrades, and the finely-carved newel posts and their highly decorative carved caps, made this sweeping staircase a delight to behold from this lowest level right up to the top of the stairs on the Boat Deck. The walls were clad in oak panelling and the stairwell was crowned with an ornate dome of opaque glass panels supported by a lattice of iron framing.

The reception area itself was elegantly furnished with comfortably upholstered sofas, a scattering of tables, cane chairs and dark carpeting covering a floor that stretched the full width of the vessel. The overall theme of the room was

intended to be Jacobean, with bronze wall lights casting patterns on the white-painted wood panelling and a white plaster ceiling where further electric lights gave the room a very bright and airy feel. This was the area designed for first-class passengers to congregate and relax with cocktails before sitting down to dinner. Revolving doors lead them through into the main first-class dining saloon. Again stretching the full width of the ship and running to 114 feet (35 metres) in length, this room was the largest public area on the ship. More than 550 diners could be served at any one sitting. The White Star Line described it as:

An immense room decorated in a style peculiarly English, reminiscent of early Jacobean times; but instead of the sombre oak of the sixteenth and seventeenth centuries, it is painted a soft, rich white, which, with the coved and richly-moulded ceilings and the spacious character of the apartment, would satisfy the most aesthetic critic. The furniture is of oak designed to harmonise with its surroundings.

Around the walls were alcoves where tables were arranged to provide diners with some privacy, while screens could be requested for an even cosier dining experience.

The central section of the dining room was designed as a dance floor and was overlooked by a raised orchestra platform. At the opposite end of the dining room from the reception area was the first-class pantry, which led on to silver, china, cutlery and glass stores before you reached the galley. Food for both the first- and second-class dining rooms was prepared here on two enormous ranges that were said to be the biggest in the world. There were 19 ovens, four silver grills, roasters, steam ovens, steam stockpots and an array of electric gadgets for slicing, carving, peeling, mincing or whisking. There were also cold stores, a bakery, a baker's shop, a butcher's shop and coal bunkers to feed the ranges' ovens.

It was here that the final first-class dinner was prepared. The menu offered hors d'oeuvres of canapés à l'amiral or oysters à la Russe, followed by a soup course of either consommé Olga or cream of barley. There was then a fish course of poached salmon before the entrées – filet mignon Lili, sauté of chicken Lyonnaise or vegetable marrow farcie. There followed a choice between lamb with mint sauce, Calvados-glazed roast duckling with apple sauce, roast sirloin of beef forestière and a selection of vegetables or rice. The menu rolled on through salad, paté, sweets and ice cream to finish with a dessert of assorted fresh fruit and cheese. Needless to say, all of this was prepared, presented and served to the sort of standard one would expect in the finest restaurants of Paris, London or New York.

Aft of the galley on the starboard side, and completely separate from the galley, was the ship's hospital with its own stair access to the floors below and above.

Directly behind the galley was the second-class pantry, the facilities of which, on a smaller scale, mirrored those in the first-class pantry. This opened into the second-class dining saloon. Diners entered this room via doors from the second-class main

stairway which, with its dark, gleaming, polished oak balustrade and matching wall panels was, if not as breathtaking as the first-class grand staircase, still of a standard to grace a country house hotel. The oak panelling on the walls of the stairway was carried through into the dining room, which again stretched the width of the ship, but at 71 feet (22 metres) long could seat only 394 diners. Despite being prepared in the same galley, the food on the second-class menu was not of the same quality as that offered to first-class diners but, while it was simpler fare, a second-class dinner would still run to six courses.

The aft exit from the second-class dining room led out on to the second of the second-class stairways, a range of second-class cabins beyond which, at the stern of D Deck, were the third-class stairway and further third-class cabin accommodation.

Above the Saloon Deck was C Deck, the Shelter Deck. Crew's mess facilities and galleys in the bow gave way to a loading well equipped with two electric cranes to service the cargo areas accessed via No 2 hatch and the bunker hatch. Aft of this cargo handling area was first-class accommodation. In fact, all of the passenger cabins from this deck upward were devoted to first class. The majority of these cabins were suites with two bedrooms and their own private bathrooms, although

the design allowed for an arrangement of interconnecting doors, offering a great deal of flexibility in the way that the suites could be sold. There was the opportunity for White Star to offer a single-bedroomed suite with its own bathroom, and then to offer the second bedroom as a private first-class cabin without bathroom.

The most desirable of the suites were the state rooms, which could be booked with a room to be used as a drawing room, sitting room or even a private dining room. The sitting rooms were decorated in a most elaborate manner, mimicking the grandeur of a number of different styles and periods. There were rooms in the style of Louis XV, Renaissance, Georgian, Queen Anne, Empire, Adam, Modern Dutch and Old Dutch. They were appointed with the finest quality furnishings that suited the period and the walls were panelled with polished oak, mahogany or sycamore. To fit with the intended style – Adam, for example – the wall panels were painted accordingly, as were the decorative plaster mouldings on the ceilings. Nowhere in any of these rooms would there be found any bare pipe or steelwork to betray the fact that this was actually a cabin aboard ship. The rooms even had mantelpieces above appropriately styled fireplaces to complete the effect. The beds were of brass, mahogany or oak, larger than in standard

Above left: The Promenade Deck, where first-class passengers could stroll, take the air and enjoy the sea views while remaining under the protection of the Boat Deck above.

Above right: The first-class Grand Staircase allowed passengers to make an elegant entrance to the reception room on D Deck leading to the first-class dining room, where groups would gather prior to going in to dinner. The Grand Staircase was capped at Boat Deck level with an ornate glass dome.

cabins, and had reading lights on the wall above the bedhead to complement the other electric wall and ceiling lights. Some were also equipped with electric ceiling fans and electric heaters.

Around the area of the grand staircase were the enquiry office and the purser's office, while moving aft from the grand staircase there were suites to port and starboard with smaller standard first-class cabins on the inboard sides of the port and starboard corridors. It was envisaged that many of these cabins would be occupied by the servants of the first-class passengers travelling in the more expensive suites, and to that end provision was also made for a 'Maids and Valets' saloon. The first-class barber's shop was also in this section and on the starboard side, above the hospital, was the first-class surgery.

Aft of the first-class section was the second-class promenade, an enclosed area of deck protected from the

elements by a solid bulwark fitted with a long row of large windows. This promenade was also one of the second-class entrance areas, there being another two decks below on E Deck and one up above on B Deck. Between the port and starboard promenades was another of the ship's most lavishly decorated spaces, the second-class library. The library had sycamore wood panelling on the walls with a mahogany dado rail and mahogany furnishings. A large bookcase adorned the forward wall while the bulkheads to the promenades outside had large windows draped with silk curtains. A Wilton carpet helped to maintain this as a retreat of peace and quiet.

The aft part of the enclosed port and starboard promenades included separate areas for 'tourist' or third-class sheltered promenades, opening on to the open deck area to the rear of the second-class library. This was the rear cargo-handling area, above which hung four electric cranes. The hatches here gave access all the way down to the refrigerated cargo hold on the Orlop Deck, but the deck surrounding the hatches was reserved as the first of the open deck areas available for the use of passengers – the main third-class promenade. Through two sets of doors aft of the promenade was one of the third-class entrance areas, with another directly below on D Deck and one in the bow on E Deck. Naturally, the third-class

This page: Francis Browne took this photograph of passengers being seated in the first-class dining room.

Opposite: Devoid of passengers, place settings and table cloths, the extent of the first-class dining room is more apparent in this official Harland & Wolff photograph, as is the ornate plasterwork on the ceiling.

Opposite: First-class passengers brave the elements strolling on the Promenade Deck.

Left: Another of Francis Browne's photographs, this one looking forward from the after end of the Promenade Deck. The open doors lead in to the verandah and palm court area while the passengers looking down from above are standing in the second-class promenade area on the Boat Deck.

entrances were nowhere near as grand as those enjoyed by first-class passengers. The steel girders were flanked by their rows of rivets painted stark white and the ceiling was formed not of lovingly crafted plaster mouldings but from the white-painted steel plates of the deck above. Nevertheless, this was no ordinary immigrant ship, this was the *Titanic*, and provision had been made for the 'steerage' passengers over and above that which they might expect on a lesser ship.

In the port side entrance area, a small bar was planned along with a large room taking up half the width of this stern section and designated as the third-class smoking room. This room had oak-panelled walls, teak tables and chairs, and a linoleum-covered floor, giving the impression of a large saloon bar. On the starboard side, opposite the smoking room, was another facility for third-class passengers, the common, or 'general' room. This was a bright, popular room with white-painted, pine-panelled walls and teak benches, tables and

chairs. Intended as a meeting room for socialising and relaxation, a piano stood against the back wall. The ship's musicians did not play here, but many other musicians undoubtedly did during impromptu sing-songs – not a room that would have been appreciated by the postal workers on board the *Olympic*!

The final stern compartment on C Deck was a machine space designed mainly to house the equipment for operating the steering gear and stern capstans.

The next level up from C Deck was the Bridge Deck, also called B Deck. The farthest forward part of the bow of B Deck was the forecastle where the anchor chains lay in the channels through which they ran, descending at one end into the chain lockers and at the other out through the hull to the port and starboard anchors. Despite the fact that these side anchors each weighed 8 tons, the *Titanic* was also equipped with a much larger centre anchor. The centre anchor was stowed in a cradle on the forecastle and could be deployed when required to prevent the ship from dragging its side anchors in a strong current or tide. The centre anchor weighed a colossal 50.5 tons. At the aft end of the forecastle was the forward mast. Along with its twin 600 feet (183 metres) back in the stern section, it was designed to keep the radio aerial at least 30 feet (9 metres) above the top of the funnels so that gases from the funnels would not interfere with radio reception or transmission.

Aft of the mast was the cargo handling well and then that part of Bridge Deck that was an integral part of the *Titanic's* superstructure. Here the plans included a forward promenade for first-class passengers followed by a series of first-class suites up to the area of the grand staircase, where there was another first-class entrance. Aft of this entrance were the two most desirable suites on the whole ship. One was on the starboard side and one on the port side. Each was intended to have two bedrooms, a private bathroom and two 'wardrobe' rooms (all of which could be found in many other first-class suites) plus a large sitting room and their truly unique feature – private promenade decks. Around 15 feet (4 metres) wide and 50 feet (15 metres) long, these promenades were fully enclosed with cane deck chairs and loungers in which to relax

while enjoying the view. Large windows looked out over the sea and the ceilings were fitted with fake oak beams to match the oak-framed panels on the outside walls of the suites. These were the *Titanic's* most expensive suites, costing £870, but anyone booking one was automatically given an inside first-class cabin for the use of a servant.

Travelling to New York in one of these suites was Mrs Charlotte Cardeza and her son Thomas, who boarded at Cherbourg. Mrs Cardeza's baggage included 14 trunks, four suitcases, three crates and a medicine chest. Her baggage included 70 dresses, 38 feather boas and 10 fur coats. Travelling with the Cardezas was their maid, Anna. The other promenade suite was occupied by J Bruce Ismay, his valet and secretary, but it was originally booked for J P Morgan. Morgan cancelled his trip at the eleventh hour, claiming ill-health, allowing Ismay to take over the suite that had been designed to Morgan's specifications to be reserved for his personal use whenever he wished to travel.

The first-class suites that were designed to take up the mid-ships section of B Deck were slightly less spacious than the 'promenade suites', but still lavishly appointed in one or other of the many period styles adopted aboard the *Titanic*. These ran back on the starboard side as far as what was intended to be the restaurant promenade outside the *à la carte* dining room. On the *Titanic* this actually became the Café Parisien. A popular spot with the younger first-class passengers, this area was designed to have the ambience of a pavement café with wooden trellis work on the walls – up which ivy or vines were intended to grow – and matching patterns in the woodwork on the ceiling. There were, of course, electric ceiling lights but natural light flooded in through the large windows, giving the café what was described as 'the appearance of a charming sun-lit verandah'. The cane furniture added to the outdoors look, although passengers choosing to dine here enjoyed the same standard of food and service as those in the *à la carte* restaurant.

The remainder of this section of B Deck, stretching all the way across to the port side, was devoted to the reception area, galley and pantry of the *à la carte* dining room, the dining room itself occupying the lion's share of this space. Decorated in the

style of Louis XVI, the room was panelled in a light, yet richly textured, French walnut with gilded details. The columns supporting the plaster ceiling with its delicately moulded flower patterns, were encased in carved wood, again with gilded decorative detail and a rose-coloured Axminster carpet covered the floor. Great attention to detail was paid in the design of the brass ceiling lights, door handles, hinges and general fixtures to maintain the period style, with the finely carved furniture in the same light walnut as the walls. The restaurant could seat almost 140 diners who enjoyed a menu prepared by the Italian restaurateur Luigi Gatti. Gatti ran two fashionable Ritz restaurants in London – Gatti's Adelphi and Gatti's Strand. He was offered the opportunity to run the *à la carte* restaurant as a kind of franchise and, for the *Titanic's* maiden voyage, he brought with him his own chefs, *maitre d'*, manager and waiting staff, who were mainly either French or Italian. Ten of his staff were his cousins and this was to be their first ocean voyage.

Like the main dining room, the *à la carte* restaurant had its own reception room, decorated in a Georgian style with silk-faced sofas and armchairs in which to enjoy a pre-dinner drink. Diners who chose to use the *à la carte* dining room instead of the first-class restaurant qualified for a rebate on their tickets, should those tickets have included meals, to compensate for

Left: Gym wear in 1912 was a far cry from the figure-hugging lycra of the 21st century. This couple are enjoying a leisurely cycle in front of the *Titanic's* gymnasium clock.

the fact that they were paying extra for the experience of dining at Signor Gatti's establishment.

Beyond Gatti's restaurant was an area earmarked as a second-class entrance and promenade with, between the port and starboard open areas, the second-class smoking room. The equal of any first-class public room on any other ship in the world, the *Titanic's* second-class smoking room was panelled from floor to ceiling in carved oak with oak tables and chairs, the chairs upholstered in dark green leather. The linoleum tiles on the floor had been specially designed and a fully-stocked bar occupied on corner of the room.

The cargo handling area took up the space aft of the smoking room and at the stern of B Deck was the Poop Deck. This rounded stern deck and the decks immediately below it were designed to overhang the steering gear in the style of a schooner. The Poop Deck housed the stern capstans, two electric cranes for cargo handling and a stern bridge on a raised platform that was used to help guide the ship when docking. The open deck area was also designated as a third-class promenade.

The *Titanic's* second highest deck was A Deck, the Promenade Deck. Reserved for the use of first-class passengers only, the Promenade Deck was 500 feet (152 metres) long and up to 30 feet (9 metres) wide down the port and starboard sides. Although covered by the deck plates of the Boat Deck above, most of the promenade area was open, providing uninterrupted sea views. The Promenade Deck provided one of the most obvious visible differences between the *Titanic* and *Olympic*. Perhaps as a response to comments from passengers on the *Olympic* who had complained about being buffeted by the wind and soaked by sea spray, the forward part of the promenade deck was enclosed with a steel bulwark and glass windows that could be lowered in fine weather. The forward part of A Deck, surrounded by the enclosed section of promenade, was given over to smaller first-class cabins and a first-class entrance either side of the grand staircase. Although it was not originally planned, a larger first-class cabin was also added on A Deck and, when the *Titanic* set sail for New York, this was occupied by Thomas Andrews.

Aft of the accommodation was the first-class reading room. Situated on the port side, this room's moulded wood panelling was painted white, reflecting the light from the great bay window that looked out over the promenade. Furnished with well-upholstered armchairs for reading and more upright darkwood cushioned chairs for sitting at one of the many tables to write a letter or postcard, this was considered to be very much a ladies' room. Adjacent to the reading room was the first-class lounge.

Of all the public rooms on the *Titanic*, this was the one to rival any of the world's top hotels. The polished wood panelling was adorned with exquisite carvings subtly lit by electric candelabra-style wall lights. Huge mirrors reflected light all round the room while the ornate central ceiling light helped to display the finest plaster mouldings anywhere on the ship. A magnificent fireplace with overmantel mirror stood at one end of the room, while against the opposite wall was an elaborate mahogany bookcase. Passengers could borrow books from here to take to the reading room next door or settle down on one of the many armchairs or sofas scattered around the room. There were tables for playing cards or writing, quiet alcoves for relaxed conversation and, naturally, instant steward service from a morning cup of coffee to an afternoon gin and tonic.

Beyond the pantry and bar intended to serve the lounge was the first-class smoking room. The dark mahogany panels lining the walls of this Georgian-style room were heavily carved and inlaid with mother-of-pearl. The panels surrounding the ventilation shaft that rose all the way up from the main engine room were framed ornate screens of stained glass showing sports scenes or representations of landmarks around the world where, one day, the *Titanic* might visit. Like the lounge next door, the smoking room had its own impressive fireplace and its own bar. The furniture, however, was far more robust and masculine, winged leather armchairs and leather-trimmed seats surrounding the numerous card tables. If the reading room could be described as a ladies' room, then this room was undoubtedly one for the gentlemen.

Aft of the smoking room were the verandah and palm court rooms. These areas were designed to further the impression that the *Titanic* was actually a floating country mansion. Trellis work similar to that in the Café Parisien was festooned with greenery as though these were garden rooms. Walking through the doors from the smoking room into the verandah areas was intended to be like stepping out into a conservatory. Cane furniture and tables along with linoleum tiles rather than the plush carpets in the lounge or smoking room helped to foster this illusion.

The final deck of the ship was the Boat Deck. In the forward section was the wheelhouse, the captain's cabin, officers' quarters and the Marconi radio telegraph room. It was here that the radio operator, Jack Phillips, and his junior, Harold Bride, listened for incoming messages and tapped out the Morse code signals being sent from the *Titanic* both to other ships and to shore stations within the equipment's 350-mile (563-kilometre) range. Phillips and Bride were afforded the rank of junior officers, but they were actually employees of Marconi rather than members of the ship's crew.

The top of the great glass dome, inside which was suspended a glittering crystal chandelier, occupied the central deck space aft of the officers' quarters. Beyond that was another of the *Titanic's* unique first-class facilities – the gymnasium. Situated on the starboard side of No 2 funnel, the

gymnasium was panelled in plain white, the walls unadorned except for a map of the world showing White Star Line routes, an illustration of the *Titanic* with a deck guide and a large clock face. The gym boasted the most modern equipment. Some, such as the weights machines, rowing machines and cycling machines would be immediately recognisable to anyone who uses a gym today. Other machines such as the electric camel and electric horse might not be quite so familiar. Ladies could use the gym from 9.00am until 1.00pm, and gentleman from 2.00pm until 6.00pm. Children were allowed in from 1.00pm until 3.00pm. A visit to the gymnasium cost one shilling and, while exercising, passengers would be supervised by the *Titanic's* fitness instructor, Mr Thomas W McCauley.

The remainder of the central section of the Boat Deck was taken up by the raised roof over the first-class lounge, on top of which was an isolated brass platform. Here one of the ship's compasses was kept free from any magnetic interference that might be caused by the iron and steel of the ship's structure. There was an officers' mess and other crew facilities, storage and the raised roof over the first-class smoking room. One of the storage areas at the base of No 4 funnel was designed to be kennels for those travelling with their pet dogs. Along the port and starboard sides of the deck were promenades for the

Above left: Francis Browne took this shot of the first-class reading and writing room on the Promenade Deck.

Above right: Taking some exercise on the port side of the Boat Deck, the rear section of which was reserved for second-class passengers.

officers, first-class promenades amidships and second-class promenades to the stern.

The real purpose of the Boat Deck, of course, was for the boats. The boat deck was originally intended to take 48 or even 64 lifeboats, but this number was reduced to give more space for the promenade areas and to avoid giving the impression that the ship was overloaded with lifeboats. Passengers were being assured that the Titanic was the most modern, safest ship afloat. Why then undermine their confidence by crowding the upper decks with lifeboats? The ultimate designs showed eight first-class lifeboats (and two small cutters) forward, and eight second-class lifeboats aft. The four Englehardt collapsible liferafts brought the total number of lifeboats on the Titanic to 20. The total lifeboat capacity was 1,176 – only enough for around one-third of the 3,300 passengers and crew who could be carried on the Titanic when she was fully booked.

The Titanic's design, even though she was the sister ship to the Olympic, was unique, as was the Olympic's, given the detailed differences between them. The Titanic was undoubtedly the most luxurious liner ever to put to sea, but at least some elements of her interior décor would have looked a little familiar to seasoned travellers. The interior design of many liners at that time was remarkably similar as adaptations of the same concept drawings would be used on different projects. Not all of the design work on the interiors was executed in-house by Harland & Wolff and the interior design contractors would certainly modify their drawings for the Titanic and then use them on other projects for which they were commissioned, just as the drawings for the Titanic and the Olympic may have been adaptations of earlier work. The materials used and the styles would echo earlier work.

Regardless of any such minor points, the White Star Line considered that Harland & Wolff had produced a package that met J P Morgan's demand for the 'finest vessels afloat' when J Bruce Ismay visited Belfast to review the drawings on 29 July 1908. After a formal presentation of the designs, he gave his approval and a contract was signed for the construction of the first two Olympic-class ships – Harland & Wolff keel numbers 400 (Olympic) and 401 (Titanic).

The *Titanic*'s hull begins to emerge from the scaffolding as she rests on Harland & Wolff's No 3 slipway below the giant Arrol Gantry. Riveting her 30ft- (9 metre) long hull plates to her framing skeleton took seven months and was completed in October 1910.

WHITE STAR
ROYAL MAIL STEAMER
"TITANIC"

THE SHIPS
TAKE SHAPE

Right: The Thompson Graving dock was completed by the Belfast Port Authority just in time to take the new White Star liners *Olympic* and *Titanic*. The new dock cost around £350,000 and 500 men were employed in its construction, but without it there would have been nowhere in Belfast big enough to take the new liners in order to complete the dry dock phase of their construction. The dock is still in regular use almost a century later.

The first problem shipbuilders face when they decide to construct the biggest ships the world has ever seen is where to build them? Obviously, the *Titanic* and *Olympic* were to be built by Harland & Wolff in Belfast. But were there facilities in Ulster big enough for the building of these massive liners? Could Harland & Wolff really cope with such an immense project? Moreover, once the ships were launched, when they left Belfast to enter service, would any port be capable of accommodating them?

In Belfast, preparations for the construction of bigger ships had actually been underway for many years. It was obvious to anyone involved in shipbuilding that ship owners were always going to demand bigger and better vessels. The Belfast Harbour Commission had long benefited from the advice of senior executives at Harland & Wolff. Sir Edward Harland had, after all, been its chairman and Lord Pirrie had also served on the commission. Along with Gustav Wolff, they had both also been deeply committed to local politics, putting themselves in strategically advantageous positions to encourage the authorities in Belfast to provide the most modern facilities possible in order to promote the all-important local shipbuilding industry.

Some would have it that Harland & Wolff 'bullied' Belfast's local authorities into doing whatever they wished. Certainly, had

there been any lack of co-operation, Lord Pirrie would have been bullish enough to point out that Harland & Wolff could just as easily build ships on the Clyde or the Tyne as they could on the Lagan. That would mean the loss of 15,000 Belfast jobs – plus those involved in ancillary or support industries. It is more charitable to assume, however, that the authorities in Belfast regarded the commercial wellbeing of Harland & Wolff and the livelihoods of many Belfast families to be so closely linked that whatever was good for Harland & Wolff was good for Belfast. The decision, therefore, of the Belfast Harbour Commissioners in 1902 to create a new dry dock bigger than any that had previously been built should come as no real surprise. The meeting between Lord Pirrie and J Bruce Ismay in Downshire House, where they sketched out plans for their Olympic-class ships, was still four years away, but bigger ships were definitely on the cards and Belfast needed to be able to compete with rival shipbuilding towns. In the end, the new dry dock would still be a fairly tight squeeze for the *Titanic* and *Olympic*.

Belfast's new facility was to be called the Thompson Graving Dock and contracts for its construction were issued in 1903, the three-and-a-half-year work schedule due to commence within a year. A civil engineering company from London – Walter, Scott & Middleton – was drafted in as the main contractor, although local Belfast firms were also involved in the

Left: The *Titanic* was registered in Liverpool, although she was destined never to visit that port. The White Star Line maintained its headquarters in Liverpool, but had moved its base of operations for the transatlantic trade to Southampton, from where the *Titanic* would set sail on her doomed maiden voyage.

£350,000 project (in today's terms it would be worth about £50–100 million), which at one time employed around 500 men. The dry dock was 128 feet (39 metres) wide at the top and 850 feet (259 metres) long, with a special outer door that could extend the overall length of the dock to over 887 feet (270 metres). Without that special provision, the *Titanic* and *Olympic* would not have fitted in. Millions of tons of concrete, brick and granite stonework were used to build the dock that had a floor and walls almost 20 feet (6 metres) thick. When it was flooded, 23 million gallons (105 million litres) of water poured in but the dock's steam-powered pumps could empty all of that out again in less than three hours. The centre of the dock's floor was laid with cast iron keel plates that were topped with timber.

When a ship entered the dry dock, or graving dock (so-called because its shape resembled a grave), the gates would close behind it and the water would be pumped out in stages. The ship's keel would then settle on the keel plates and as the pumps evacuated the rest of the water, props would be wedged between the ship's hull and the walls of the dock to hold it steady. Repairs and maintenance to the hull or finishing work on a newly-launched ship could then be carried out. Because the nearby Alexandra Dry Dock had collapsed mainly as a result of the work being done on the new Thompson Graving Dock, the project took almost twice as long to complete as expected, and the very first ship to enter the dock was the *Olympic* on 1 April 1911.

Hugely expensive dredging operations were also undertaken in the river opposite the Thompson Graving Dock to provide a depth of water that would allow bigger ships to be manoeuvred in through the gates. Lord Pirrie knew that there would be a dry dock in Belfast for his new ships once they were launched, but what about their actual construction? How was Harland & Wolff to cope with the construction of these giants?

Harland & Wolff at Queen's Island consisted in 1908 of four areas: the Musgrave, Queen's, Abercorn and Victoria Shipyards. To provide for the building of the new ships, Lord Pirrie proposed that the three slipways in the Queen's Yard be demolished and replaced with two larger ones side by side. A third, smaller, auxiliary slipway was subsequently added during the building of the main two. The smaller slip became No 1 slipway; the others Nos 2 and 3. An enormous steel gantry crane system was planned to straddle the two main slipways.

Designed to specifications prepared by Harland & Wolff staff, the contract for the building of the gantry system eventually went to the Glasgow engineering company of Sir William Arrol. Arrol had built the Tay Rail Bridge, which was completed in 1887 (replacing the one that had collapsed so disastrously in 1879), and the Forth Rail Bridge, which opened in 1890. He had also been involved in the construction of London's Tower Bridge. The Arrol Gantry that was to span the Queen's Yard slipways Nos 2 and 3 was a latticework of steel supported by three rows of 11 steel-girder columns. Almost 270 feet (82 metres) wide and 840 feet (256 metres) long, the gantry reached a height of 228 feet (69 metres). It was topped by a number of crane systems, including three moving frames over each slipway and was served by four elevators as well as numerous walkways. This complex, 6,000-ton steel structure would dominate the Belfast skyline until it was eventually dismantled in the 1960s. The gantry was completed in good time for the laying of the *Olympic's* keel on No 2 slipway on 16 December 1908.

Even though Harland & Wolff were committed to building the first two Olympic-class liners, other work at their complex continued. Of the 15,000 men the company employed, the construction of the *Olympic* and *Titanic* required no more than 4,000 each. The remaining workers were involved in other projects, not least the building of the White Star Line tenders,

On No 2 slipway, work continues on the plating of the *Olympic*'s Tank Top with her stern framing takes shape at the far end of the gantry. Part of the *Titanic*'s bottom can be seen to the left on No 3 slipway.

the *Nomadic* and *Traffic*. These two ships, each around ̱20 feet (67 metres) long, were destined to work in the French port of Cherbourg in Normandy.

The White Star Line maintained its headquarters in Liverpool but had moved its base of operations for the transatlantic trade to Southampton. While they were both registered in Liverpool (the *Titanic*, in fact, was destined never to visit Liverpool), the *Olympic* and *Titanic* would sail from Southampton, calling at Cherbourg and Queenstown before heading out across the Atlantic to New York. The port facilities at Southampton could adequately accommodate the world's two largest ships, but their next port of call, Cherbourg, could not. Too big to approach the quayside, the liners would have to anchor offshore while the *Nomadic* and *Traffic* carried passengers, baggage and mail to and fro. The *Nomadic* was to carry the first-class and second-class passengers, while the *Traffic* carried third-class travellers, baggage and mail. The same situation prevailed at the ships' second port of call, Queenstown, where the tenders the *America* and *Ireland* would service the liners.

At their ultimate destination, New York, the White Star Line had requested that the port authorities enlarge the piers to allow the new ships to dock, but the request had been denied on the grounds that extending out into the Hudson River would constitute a danger to navigation. That danger suddenly evaporated when pressure was brought to bear on the authorities by J P Morgan. The man who could sway presidents, dominated Wall Street, ran US Steel, owned a fair portion of the railroads and planned a monopoly in transatlantic trade was not about to let the City of New York's Port Authority stand in his way. White Star's superliners would have docking facilities in New York.

No problem, it seemed, could stand in the way of the construction of the *Olympic* and *Titanic*. Four months after work began on the *Olympic* the keel of Harland & Wolff ship 401, the *Titanic*, was laid below the giant gantry on No 3 slip.

The keel is the spine of the ship, the main member from which the rest of the ship's structure will grow. The *Titanic's* keel was made up of a central hollow steel box girder over 5 feet (1.5 metres) deep, mounted on a steel keel plate and

Above: The *Olympic's* keel was laid on 16 December 1908, four months ahead of the *Titanic*, although the *Titanic* would eventually be launched more than seven months after her sister ship.

reinforcing solid steel bar. Further girders ran either side of this 'spine' to create the bottom of the *Titanic's* hull with steel cross-members linking the girders. This entire framework was riveted together mechanically, using massive hydraulic pincers and half a million rivets – the rivets alone weighed 270 tons in total. Steel plates 1 inch (2.5 centimetres) thick were riveted to the bottom, sides and top of the frame. The 'double bottom' thus formed was seen as a major safety feature – should the bottom plates be breached, water would only penetrate as far as the top plates.

The cross-member beams had circular channels cut through them to create a honeycomb of compartments, or tanks, within the double bottom of the ship, although some were solid to create separations between the tanks. These tanks would be filled with water ballast to a greater or lesser degree when the *Titanic* set sail. Ballast is necessary to make a ship ride in the water at the right height. A lightly laden ship will sit higher in the water and be susceptible to the forces of the wind and waves, and so be more liable to bob around. To ensure a smoother passage, the ship takes on ballast that will allow it to sit lower in the water and thus be more stable. As the *Titanic* set out across the Atlantic, burning over 600 tons of coal per day and with food and fresh water stores also being consumed, she would become lighter and ballast would have to be taken on to maintain her stability. Ballast could be pumped between tanks, if required, to balance evenly the weight of the water, while bilge keel tanks 300 feet (91 metres) long to the port and starboard helped to stop the sideways rolling of the ship in heavy seas. With its plating all in place, this entire structure became the Tank Top.

From the bottom of the ship grew the side frames, the ship's ribs. Each was over 60 feet (18 metres) high, and they were spaced at 3-foot (91-centimetre) intervals along the length of the ship. At the bow and stern the spacing was reduced even further. At each deck level, the deck beams were attached to the framing ribs and cross-beams were also added. These beams were 10 inches (25 centimetres) deep up to Lower Deck level, but slightly smaller above that to prevent the ship becoming top heavy. The cross-beams were supported by solid steel stanchions and pillars to make the entire framework of the ship an immensely strong grid of interconnected boxes. This was precision engineering, careful and methodical work that took over a year until the *Titanic* was fully framed in early April 1910. The plating of the hull could then begin.

The plates used on the *Titanic* were 30 feet (9 metres) long by 6 feet (1.8 metres) wide and 1 inch (2.5 centimetres) thick. On the upper decks, the deck plating used was even thicker to increase the strength of the hull. The plates were attached to the framing along the ship's sides in strips called 'strakes' and overlapped in a series of 'joggles' when they were riveted together. This overlapping meant that the plates on the *Titanic's* hull resembled the slates on the roof of a house. Today, the hull plates of a ship are butted together and welded for a smooth, streamlined finish, but in 1910 there was no alternative to riveting. The seams of the plates were double-riveted while the butts were treble- or quadruple-riveted for extra strength, especially on the bottom plating. Once the riveters had finished their work, the caulkers turned their attention to key joints. On an old-fashioned wooden sailing ship, caulking had meant hammering tarred rope into gaps between the ship's planking or decking to make it watertight. On the *Titanic*, the caulker's job was to force a special putty into vulnerable joints using a high-pressure hydraulic pump.

By 19 October 1910, all of *Titanic's* hull plates had been hammered into place and the following day the *Olympic*, still several months ahead of her sister ship, was launched from No

2 slipway. Although her plating was completed, the *Titanic* had some way to go before she was ready for launching. Certain sections of the hull would be pumped full of water to check they were watertight on the basis that if they could hold water in, they could keep water out. Just before the *Titanic's* keel had been laid orders were issued to the engine works for the manufacture of her boilers to commence. Subsequent instructions were issued as the hull took shape for other essential components and a steady stream of components now began to arrive at No 3 slipway, either from other parts of the Harland & Wolff complex or from outside manufacturers. The 15-ton stem anchor was delivered by local hauliers, John Harkness & Co, on a steel-wheeled wagon pulled by a team of 20 horses. Each of the two side anchors weighed around 8 tons and each link of their massive chains was 175 pounds (79 kilograms).

Specially cast steel brackets were delivered from the Darlington Forge Company to house the propeller shafts. The brackets for the port and starboard propellers held the shafts clear of either side of the hull and were plated over, forming streamlined 'wings'. The central propeller shaft housing was situated further astern than the two wing propellers and formed part of the sternpost casting that supported the ship's rudder. The sternpost was the 'hinge' on which the rudder 'door' pivoted to steer the ship. The central propeller turned immediately in front of the rudder, making the steering more effective as its thrust was deflected by the huge rudder. Also cast by the Darlington Forge, the rudder was manufactured in six segments which, when fully assembled, created a blade 78 feet 8 inches (23 metres) high and 15 feet 3 inches (4 metres) at its widest.

The rudder was hung on the stern post below the overhang of the Poop Deck, Shelter Deck and the sternmost part of the Saloon Deck. The steering gear required to turn the rudder was housed on the Shelter Deck and was, like all of the *Titanic's* equipment, built to a formidable scale. Even the rudder stock – the 'axle' turned by the machinery – was enormous at almost 2 feet (60 centimetres) in diameter. The steering gear was powered by two three-cylinder engines, although either engine

The two sister ships grow side by side at Harland & Wolff's Queen's Yard. The height of the Arrol Gantry and the bulk of the ships it enclosed made them the dominant feature of the landscape for miles around.

was capable of doing the job alone and one was generally maintained as a standby. The machinery could be controlled either from the wheelhouse or from the docking bridge platform above the Poop Deck.

The propeller shaft housing formed part of the *Titanic's* hull and, like the rudder, some of the engine equipment and other essential fittings were installed while the ship was still on No 3 slipway. When a ship is launched, it is far from complete – more an empty shell than a finished vessel – but the deck beams and plating form an integral element of the hull's strength and have to be finished to a certain degree before the hull hits the water. Clearly manoeuvring some of the *Titanic's* bulkier equipment into place with so much of the structure already built would have been impossible, so some equipment was part-assembled and 'sealed in' as construction progressed. It would have been equally impractical to install all of the *Titanic's* fixtures and fittings, especially the complete superstructure, funnels and masts, while she rested on the slipway. So, like every other ship, the *Titanic* would go to a fitting-out dock and then into a dry dock for finishing, subsequent to her launch.

The *Olympic* spent seven months after her launch being completed and fitted out. By that time, the *Titanic* was ready to be launched and Lord Pirrie decided that, unlike Harland & Wolff's usual ship launches, which were rather subdued events, the *Titanic's* would be a very special occasion. On 29 May 1911, the *Olympic* was due to leave Belfast for two days of sea trials in order to be certified by the Board of Trade as seaworthy and fit to carry passengers. Before she left, the *Olympic* was opened to the public and thousands queued to take a look round the luxury liner, paying up to 5 shillings for the privilege – a day's wages – all of which went to local hospital charities. When the *Olympic* returned fully certified, she was to stand as a spectator to the launch of her sister ship, the *Titanic*, which was attended by the new White Star tenders the *Nomadic* and *Traffic*.

The launch of the *Titanic* was advertised by the Harbour Commission in the local newspaper and the public was invited to buy tickets for a specially reserved area at the Albert Quay that provided a perfect vantage point for the proceedings. The

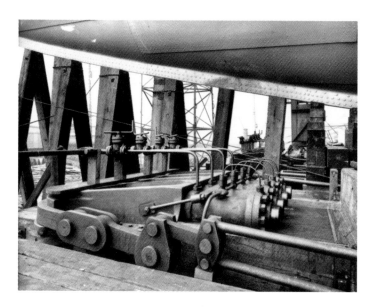

Above: The wooden props supporting the *Titanic's* hull on No 3 slipway had to be knocked away in sequence as part of the launch process before the ship could be released to slide into the water. This was dangerous work and, despite the use of hydraulic rams or triggers to hold the hull in place, making the props easier to remove, one worker died when some of the timbers collapsed on top of him.

shilling each ticket holder paid was again donated to local hospitals and tickets could be purchased at numerous shops around Belfast. It was not expected, however, that these would be the only spectators. Extra trams were laid on by the city corporation to cope with the crowds making their way down to the quaysides. Ferries and small steamers were running sightseeing trips out to the *Olympic*, anchored in Belfast Lough, and as the morning of 31 May wore on, crowds estimated at up to 100,000 gathered on the banks of the Lagan.

With the launch scheduled for 12.15pm spectators with special Harland & Wolff invitations took their seats in the three purpose-built grandstands inside the shipyard. One of these stands was reserved for the scores of journalists who attended the launch, some having travelled all the way from America. The other two were for Harland & Wolff white-collar staff and guests of the company. A further grandstand, the owners' gallery, had been built for Lord Pirrie's most distinguished guests who included Mr and Mrs McMordie, the Lord Mayor of Belfast and his Lady Mayoress; Thomas Andrews of Harland & Wolff; Mr Sanderson, a senior executive with the White Star Line; J Bruce Ismay and his family and the *Titanic's* ultimate owner – who had travelled from America just for this event – J P Morgan.

As befitting the grandest, most modern ship in the world, the *Titanic* was to be launched using the world's most modern launch system. Unlike the usual system, where all of the wooden props and supports that held the ship in place on the slipway were knocked away, albeit in a set order, until the ship moved off down the slipway, the *Titanic* was held in place by hydraulic rams or 'triggers'. These triggers took the strain off the props, making them easier and safer to remove before the triggers were released and the *Titanic* would slide gracefully into the water. To ensure that she actually did slide, the slipway was lubricated with 22 tons of a tallow-and-oil mixture.

At noon, with Lord Pirrie having left his guests to tour the slipway, check that the props had been removed and inspect the trigger mechanisms, a rocket was fired to warn any small craft in the vicinity that the *Titanic's* launch was imminent and they should stay well clear. The *Titanic* flew a red flag from her stern as a further warning. Up on top of the Arrol Gantry more cheerful flags were flying. The Union Jack and the Stars and Stripes flanked the White Star Line's red pennant with its white star, while a set of signal flags spelt out the message 'Good Luck'. At 12.10pm a second rocket was fired as a five-minute warning and to signal that Harland & Wolff's gates were closing and that no one else would be allowed in. Finally, Lord Pirrie ordered the third and final rocket to be fired and the triggers were released. There was no bottle of champagne smashed over *Titanic's* bow to christen her, no naming speech, no fuss. She simply set off on her first voyage – which lasted all of 62 seconds. Two sets of drag chains weighing 80 tons each, and special anchors (not the *Titanic's* own) buried in the riverbed

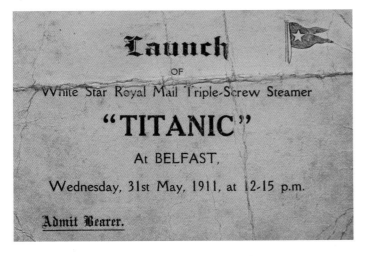

and attached via steel hawsers to eyeplates riveted to the *Titanic's* hull, slowed the ship from around 12 knots to a complete standstill before she had travelled more than half her own length.

As the cheers of the crowd subsided and the spectators began to make their way home, lunch was served for Lord Pirrie's most distinguished guests in the Harland & Wolff boardroom at Queen's Island. The gentlemen of the press and other lesser guests were entertained with a lavish lunch at the Central Hotel in Royal Avenue, Belfast. At 2.30pm, the *Nomadic* delivered a small group of passengers that included Lord Pirrie, J Bruce Ismay, J P Morgan and Thomas Andrews (as head of the Guarantee Group) to RMS *Olympic*, which left Belfast later that afternoon headed for Liverpool. Anchored in the Mersey, the *Olympic* would once again play host to an inquisitive public before setting sail for Southampton and her first Atlantic crossing.

The *Titanic*, meanwhile, was detached from her chains and anchor hawsers to be ushered to her fitting-out quay by five tugs. Four of the tugs, the *Alexandra*, *Hornby*, *Herculaneum* and *Wallasey*, came from Liverpool's Alexandra Towing Company, while the fifth, the *Hercules*, was Harland & Wolff's own vessel. At the fitting-out quay was another new Harland & Wolff acquisition. The company had bought a floating crane second-hand from Germany (which came with German workers

This photograph shows work being carried out on the *Titanic*'s starboard propeller shaft and was taken by Robert J Welch for Harland & Wolff. In order better to show the dimensions of the shaft and to balance the photograph more evenly, the photographer has doctored the photographic negative to remove one of the workmen who was standing second from the right. This created a 'ghost' image.

When the *Olympic* was launched in October 1910, she was the first of White Star's planned three new superliners and the largest ship afloat. To show her off and ensure that she looked suitably impressive, she was painted white so that she would be clearly seen against the backdrop of the Arrol Gantry and the *Titanic*. The *Olympic* was later painted black like the *Titanic*.

At her own launch on 31 May 1911, the *Titanic* was painted black and is seen here being manoeuvred towards the fitting-out quay.

to erect it and operate it while local men were trained – something that caused a great deal of friction in the shipyard) to help install some of the heavy equipment on the *Olympic* and *Titanic*. The 200-ton crane could lift a weight of 150 tons up to 150 feet (45 metres) in the air and was essential for installing items such as the *Titanic's* boilers.

Slowly, the mighty engines took shape. The *Titanic's* two conventional engines were of the triple expansion type, which meant that the steam from the boilers was used three times. Steam entered the first, smallest cylinder, a mere 4 feet 4 inches (1.3 metres) in diameter, at high pressure and expanded, pushing down the piston inside the cylinder before escaping and being fed into the second, larger, cylinder. There it would expand again and the process was repeated. The pistons pushed down to turn a crankshaft, which then turned the propeller shaft with the equivalent of 15,000 horse power – the same sort of power that might be produced by around 100 engines of the type used in a fast modern saloon car. This was enough to turn the three-blade propeller about 16 feet (5 metres) round 75 times a minute.

When the steam left the third cylinder, it was channelled into the *Titanic's* turbine engine, causing the turbine blades to spin and turn the central propeller shaft. The 16,000 horse power output from the turbine could turn the central four-blade propeller, which was cast like the others in solid manganese bronze, at 135 revolutions per minute. All of this power would give the *Titanic* a service speed of just over 21 knots, with a top speed of up to 25 knots.

As the engineers and fitters worked on the *Titanic's* power plant, electrical engineers and electricians poured over her mass of electrical fittings. Electricity came from the *Titanic's* four 400-kilowatt generators and was distributed via hundreds of miles of wiring to more electrical equipment than had ever been fitted to any ship. There were 150 electric motors powering equipment such as ventilation fans, eight electric cranes, 10,000 lamps, 1,500 electric bells for passengers to summon stewards, illuminated signs in first- and second-class corridors, 520 electric heaters, irons, hot-plates and other kitchen equipment. On the Shelter Deck just forward of the first class entrance there was an internal telephone exchange with 50 lines. The elevators used electricity as did various service lifts in the pantries, and even the ship's whistles were electrically operated.

Also operable at the flick of a switch were the *Titanic's* watertight doors. These were installed in the bulkheads running across the ship's lower decks that divided the hull into 16 watertight compartments. This was a safety feature which, in the case of a serious accident when the hull was breached, would stop water from flooding into the whole ship. If water penetrated the hull, it would be confined to the compartment that had suffered the damage and the *Titanic* was designed to stay afloat even if two compartments were completely flooded.

This was not a new idea, as Brunel had installed watertight compartments on his *Great Eastern* and *Great Britain* more than 60 years before. The trouble with watertight bulkheads, however, is that they form dead ends in corridors. Doors in the bulkheads, especially doors acceptable for use by passengers, form weak points where water will ultimately break through. But blank bulkhead walls across corridors on passenger decks are a major inconvenience. The White Star Line could not contemplate having its passengers being forced to climb stairways up to the deck above the bulkheads when trying to find their way around the ship. It was decided, therefore, that the watertight bulkheads would extend up from the Tank Top only as far as was practical. The lowest bulkhead reached only to the Middle Deck, the first deck wholly above the water line.

In the lowest part of the ship, the crew needed to be able to move from one compartment to another, particularly down in the boiler and engine rooms, and this is where the watertight doors were fitted. These were no ordinary hinged doors, but heavy portcullis-like structures based on a design developed by the German shipping line Norddeutscher-Lloyd. They were suspended above the doorways and would drop down into position, with hydraulic assistance if necessary, when the captain ordered the switch to be operated on the bridge. An electric alarm bell would then sound to warn that the doors were closing, a process that normally took 20 or 30 seconds. Crew members could also operate the doors using a hydraulic

Above: One of the watertight doors that were fitted in the *Titanic*. When open, the heavy steel door was held in position above the doorway but at the flick of a switch on the Bridge seven decks above, the door would drop down into place. It would also operate automatically should water in the compartment flood the floor to a certain level.

drinking water available from taps or fountains throughout the ship and, ironically, for the making of ice.

The work gangs labouring on every part of the ship worked on specific tasks with specialists such as carpenters or cabinet makers who had manufactured banister rails or wood panelling coming aboard to install the pieces that they had made in Harland & Wolff's workshops. There was a 'builder's specification book' running to over 300 pages that was used as a guide for the furnishing and decoration of the ship. The guide was divided into sections covering areas such as 'Castings, Decks, Lockers, Doors and Bulwarks' or 'Plumber Work', 'Ventilation and Heating' and 'Cementing and Painting'. The guide was not followed slavishly. Harland & Wolff's foremen were masters of quality control and used their experience and authority to ensure that their tradesmen finished every job – from a simple area of paintwork to the most elaborate carving or the installation of a stained glass window – to the very highest of standards.

Great care was also taken with the more bulky installations such as the ship's four colossal funnels. These left Harland & Wolff's workshops fully assembled and were transported to the fitting-out quay where they lay in specially constructed cradles sitting on railroad bogeys. These ran on the network of tramlines that criss-crossed the shipyard. A steam engine, also running on the tramlines, pulled the heavily laden bogeys at crawling pace to the quayside. There, the giant floating crane plucked the funnels off their cradles, whereupon they were delicately swung into a vertical position before being lifted high above the *Titanic* and lowered onto the Boat Deck.

With autumn approaching and work progressing at a satisfactory pace, J Bruce Ismay proposed that the *Titanic's* maiden voyage should be set for the early spring of 1912. At that point it seemed that there would be no problem in completing the *Titanic* in time and the White Star Line duly announced on 18 September 1911 the sailing date of 20 March 1912 for their latest superliner. Two days later the plan was scrapped. The *Olympic* had been involved in a fracas off the Isle of Wight and was coming home to Belfast with her tail between her legs.

lever system, and an emergency closing system was fitted that would activate when water on the deck reached a certain level. A float would rise with the water until it tripped a switch that closed the doors. This system of watertight doors and compartments, along with the double bottom and the extremely robust construction of the ship led the press and the public to dub the *Titanic* 'unsinkable', although this was not a claim ever openly made either by Harland & Wolff or the White Star Line.

Work on the *Titanic* continued at a frantic pace throughout the summer of 1911. The upper superstructure, which included the bridge and the wheel house, officers' quarters, gymnasium and the raised roofs over the first-class public areas and the grand staircase, all took shape while below decks more equipment, such as the two refrigeration engines in the port engine room were installed. These units powered the refrigerated holds that were used for perishable cargo on the Orlop Deck, as well as the food stores on the Lower Deck and the various cold stores or larders in the galley and bar areas on higher decks. The system also allowed for the cooling of

Lord Pirrie, Chairman of Harland & Wolff (left) is pictured here with Captain Edward John Smith on the deck of the *Olympic*. Captain Smith commanded the *Olympic* before taking charge of the *Titanic*.

DELAYED
DEPARTURE

On 20 September 1911, as the Royal Navy cruiser HMS *Hawke* was approaching Egypt Point on the Isle of Wight and heading up the Solent towards Portsmouth, her captain, Commander William Frederick Blunt, and his crew were observing the approach of the world's largest ocean liner, RMS *Olympic*. Roughly six times the size of the 7,500-ton *Hawke*, the *Olympic* made a fine sight as she began to pick up speed in the Solent. Having left her berth in Southampton at 11.25am with 1,313 passengers, the *Olympic* manoeuvred into the Solent at the Calshot Spit buoy at 12.34pm. A few minutes later she began to slow from around 19 knots to 11 knots in order to turn to port at the West Bramble Buoy, and thus avoid the dangerous sandbank for which it was a marker.

As the two ships drew near it became clear that the *Olympic* and *Hawke* were attempting to navigate the same channel. It was equally clear that there was not enough room for them to do so. Commander Blunt ordered a course change as the two ships were then running parallel to one another at a distance that was becoming alarmingly close. The *Olympic* then began to pick up speed again. At this point it seems that the *Hawke's* wheel jammed just as an attempt was being made to steer her away from the *Olympic* and she veered closer to the White Star ship instead. The *Hawke* was then caught in the wash from the *Olympic's* bows and dragged towards the giant liner.

Every ship as it cuts through the water creates a kind of vortex to port and starboard, the water that is pushed aside by its bows rushing back in again towards the stern. With the *Hawke* only a few hundred feet off the *Olympic's* starboard side, less than a ship's length to the *Olympic*, a collision became inevitable. The *Hawke's* bow slammed into the *Olympic's* side, making a horrendous noise on impact and slicing two great gashes in her plating towards the stern, one above the water line and one below. The steel of the *Hawke's* entire bow section crumpled like tinfoil and for a moment it looked as if she might capsize. As if by a miracle, she remained upright. Both captains had ordered their watertight doors to be closed and, while both ships were severely battered, they both looked as if they would remain afloat.

Who was to blame for the accident? With the *Hawke* having rammed the *Olympic*, at first it certainly looked as if Commander Blunt would be held responsible for causing the collision. But a subsequent naval inquiry laid the blame squarely on the poor navigation of the *Olympic*. The inquiry, however, was still some way off as HMS *Hawke* limped into Portsmouth where she would be repaired. The *Olympic* anchored off Osborne Bay, where her passengers disembarked by tender to the Isle of Wight. She then made her way back to Southampton where a proper assessment was made of her damage. In the end it took two weeks to effect the temporary repairs that would allow the *Olympic* to sail home to Belfast and the only dry dock big enough to accommodate her.

Alarmingly, the collision with the *Hawke* was not the only incident to mar the first few months of the *Olympic's* service. The *Olympic* had left Southampton on her maiden voyage on 14 June 1911, arriving in New York via Cherbourg and Queenstown seven days later – although she managed the measured route used to time Atlantic crossings in 5 days, 16 hours and 42 minutes at an average speed of just over 21 knots. Her arrival in New York caused something of a sensation, not only for the crowds of onlookers but also for the owners of ships berthed at the docks. As the *Olympic* made her way to the newly extended Pier 59, the turbulence from her propellers caused a number of vessels to strain at their moorings. The tug the *O L Hallenbeck* was sucked towards the *Olympic's* stern and the two ships made contact. This caused no more than a few scratches on the *Olympic's* paintwork, but the tug owners claimed their damage was far more extensive and sued the White Star Line for $10,000. White Star countersued but the whole affair ultimately petered out, the cases being dropped for lack of evidence.

The man in command of the *Olympic* during both the *Hawke* incident and the scrape with the *O L Hallenbeck* was Captain Edward John Smith. Born in Hanley, Stoke-on-Trent, in January 1850, Smith was the son of a potter and attended the Etruria British School up to the age of 13. He then went to Liverpool to pursue a seafaring career and by 1869 he was an apprentice with the shipping line Gibson & Co aboard their

Above: The *Olympic* settled in the Thompson Graving Dock, showing her mighty three-blade port propeller, which was powered by a conventional engine, and the central four-blade propeller which was turbine-driven. The three-blade starboard propeller is just visible beyond the central one.

American-built clipper, the *Senator Webber*. In 1880 he joined the White Star Line as fourth officer on the *Celtic* and by 1887 he had his own command as captain of the *Republic*. That year he married Sarah Eleanor Pennington at St Oswald's Church, Winwick, although the couple would spend little time together as Captain Smith was quickly becoming one of the White Star Line's most valued masters, in great demand for voyages not only across the Atlantic, but also on the Australian run. He went on to command 17 White Star vessels, including the *Coptic, Majestic, Baltic* and *Adriatic*. With White Star sailing from Southampton to New York rather than from Liverpool, Smith left Merseyside and relocated further south to live closer to the port from which he would most often depart. He moved into an impressively large, brick-built house called Woodhead in Winn Road, Southampton, with his wife and their young daughter, Helen.

Captain Smith's status within the White Star Line organisation grew as the years went by. He served with distinction during the Boer War, commanding troop ships bound for South Africa, and earned the right, as a captain of the Royal Naval Reserve, to fly a blue ensign – rather than the

merchant navy's red one – on any merchant vessel under his command. He became White Star's preferred commander when a new vessel was being put through its sea trials or to captain the ships on their maiden voyages and his charming good nature made him a great favourite with well-heeled passengers crossing the Atlantic. Some would even request when booking their passage to sail on a ship commanded by Captain Smith. Nor was he any less popular with his officers and crew, who were also keen to sail with the man whose rapport with his high-society passengers led to him becoming known as 'the millionaires' captain'. His crews referred to him affectionately as 'EJ' although, out of respect, not to his face. With a salary of £1,250 a year, Smith was the White Star Line's highest-paid officer and, as such, one of the highest-earning sea captains in the world.

The incidents with the *O L Hallenbeck* and *Hawke* did not reflect badly on Smith's career. Each incident had, after all, occurred when the ship was either entering or leaving port, at which point it was under the control of a local pilot. Smith's record was, in any case, as good as – if not better than – any sea captain at that time, which is why he was earmarked as the man to take charge of the *Titanic* on her maiden voyage. In October 1911, however, Captain Smith was in command of the world's largest damaged ship, heading for the Thompson Graving Dock in Belfast.

With the *Olympic* on her way north, work had to stop on the *Titanic* so that the dry dock could be flooded and she could be towed out and berthed. Because of the *Titanic's* draught she could not be removed from dry dock until high tide, to make sure that there was enough water under her keel when she was clear of the dock. The last thing anyone wanted was for her to run aground. Similarly, the *Olympic* had to wait for high tide before she could be manoeuvred into the dock. The extent of the damage and the need to get the *Olympic* back into service as quickly as possible meant that men had to be transferred from the *Titanic* to help with the repairs. Work on the *Titanic* did not grind to a halt completely, however, and even though the *Olympic* was laid up for repairs for six weeks the scheduled date of the *Titanic's* maiden voyage was delayed by only three. The White Star Line announced that she would sail from Southampton on 10 April 1912.

Throughout the autumn of 1911 and winter of 1912 work on the completion of the *Titanic* continued. More equipment and machinery was installed and tested including, in the lowest part of the ship, the pumps in the boiler rooms. Pumps were used to supply the boilers with water and to circulate the water within the boilers as well as for filling, emptying or balancing the tanks to maintain an even distribution of ballast. Housed in separate, specially constructed chambers within the boiler rooms to protect them from ash or dust that might cause them to jam, the pumps were also used to discharge the ash and dust.

Burning over 600 tons of coal a day produced several tons of ash that had to be disposed of through ash ejectors. There were two ash ejectors in each of the five main boiler rooms. Ash was shoveled into the ejector compartment, the inner door was sealed and seawater was pumped in under pressure. An outer door, to the outside of the hull, was then opened and the ash was expelled into the sea, the boiler rooms, of course, being below the water line. This was fine when the ship was way out in the Atlantic, but not so desirable in port. There the ash was shoveled into bags and winched out of the boiler rooms on special ash hoists for disposal.

While machinery was being put in place at the bottom of the ship, on the upper decks engineering works of a different kind were being incorporated into the *Titanic's* superstructure. From the Bridge Deck upwards, the ship was sliced into three sections by two expansion joints that ran the full width of the decks from port to starboard. These joints were to allow the ship to flex when riding rough seas. When the *Titanic* crested a high wave, it might happen that, momentarily, the centre section of the ship would be supported by the wave while the bow and stern stood clear of the water with no support. Gravity would then naturally cause the bow and stern to sag downwards. Alternatively, the bow and stern might be supported by waves causing the centre section to sag into a trough. The steel used in modern ship construction is designed to be flexible enough to compensate for this phenomenon, but

Above: The *Titanic* nears completion in the Thompson Graving Dock with her funnels and masts in place and the German floating crane in attendance.

the *Titanic* needed the expansion joints, literally vertical cuts through the top decks, to help her cope with the strain. The joints were patched with hinges made from leather, steel and iron to allow them move, although the deviation over the *Titanic's* entire 882 feet 9 inches (269 metres) of length might only amount to a few inches overall – certainly not enough for the passengers to notice that the ship was 'bending'.

A constant stream of material was now arriving daily at the dockside to be hoisted aboard the *Titanic*. Harkness, the Belfast hauliers, delivered heavier items at a rate of just over a shilling a ton. Other local companies were also involved in the completion of the ship. Lumber merchants Irvin & Sellars supplied timber, as did James Corry. J. Ridell & Co supplied buckets while Robert Kirk delivered firebricks. Still more firms were employed in upholstering furniture or providing soft furnishings or linen. The *Titanic* would set sail with 45,000 table napkins aboard, 25,000 fine towels, 7,500 bath towels, 15,000 single sheets, 3,000 double sheets and 6,000 tablecloths. This represents just a tiny fraction of the *Titanic's* housekeeping inventory, but shows something of the logistical operation underway during construction to ensure the ship was fully stocked as she neared completion, ready to depart on time – 45,000 table napkins can not, after all, be conjured up overnight.

Further items scheduled to arrive for fitting included door

handles, escutcheons, finger plates and other door furniture from London specialists N Burt & Co. Locks, lamps and electrical fittings came from William McGeoch of Glasgow, and beds and mattresses from the Birmingham firm of Hoskins & Sewell – although the Marshall Sanitary Mattress Co of London also supplied their 'Vi-Spring' line. All the while, an army of carpenters, decorators and plumbers toiled inside the ship. The tiles in the Turkish bath leisure suite were laid, as were the tiles for the swimming bath. Carpets fitters stretched and laid Axminsters and Wiltons over a thick underlay to soften the steel of the decks underfoot. Many of the tradesmen would never have seen such luxury before. The crystal chandeliers being hung by the electricians would cost more than the men earned in a year.

Yet still there were delays. A boiler-makers' strike during the *Titanic's* fitting out had been accommodated more or less within the schedule, but it was the demands of her older sister that were really to throw a spanner in the works. On 24 February 1912 the *Olympic* was two days out of New York heading eastbound across the Atlantic when she hit something below the surface of the water and lost one of the blades on her port propeller. It has been speculated that the *Olympic* passed over a wrecked ship, but the navigation of the liner was called into question as most large wrecks that might pose a danger to shipping are marked on charts for their avoidance. In fact, there was no chance that the *Olympic* hit an actual shipwreck as she was 750 miles (1,207 kilometres) off the Newfoundland coast and the ocean there is several thousand feet deep. The *Olympic* could have passed over any shipwreck resting on the bottom without even coming close to scraping it. In any case, had she gone over such a wreck, damage would have been caused all the way along her hull, not just to one propeller in the stern. It is more likely that she hit what was known as a derelict wreck.

A derelict was the wreck of a wooden ship – or part of the wreck – that was not resting on the bottom, but buoyant enough to be able to drift just below the surface. Such wrecks have been compared to semi-submerged logs, hanging in the water like the corpses of long-dead ships. The turbulence created by the *Olympic* passing above one of these derelicts might have been enough to disturb it, perhaps causing it to rise up and strike the port propeller before the ship could escape. Obviously, no one could have foreseen any of this happening.

Whatever the *Olympic* hit was big and solid enough to shear off a propeller blade. The blade would have been expected to break off in the event of a severe strike such as this in order to avoid buckling and causing serious damage to the hull. Losing a propeller blade would, however, have been immediately noticeable. The three-blade propeller was seriously unbalanced and the propeller shaft had to be disengaged immediately, otherwise its violent vibrations would have started to shake its mounting to pieces, again running the danger of damaging the hull. The shaft and the port engine could also have been destroyed.

The *Olympic*, again with Captain Smith in command, continued her journey to Cherbourg and Southampton at a reduced speed. Arriving in Southampton on 28 February, *Olympic's* passengers disembarked, her cargo and mail were unloaded and she sailed for Belfast the next day with a reduced crew; non-essential crew members such as restaurant staff, stewards, galley crew and certain of the seamen were paid off in Southampton. They would be re-hired when repairs were completed – if they had not taken the opportunity to join another ship.

The *Olympic* arrived in Belfast on 1 March to find the *Titanic* still occupying the dry dock. With the next high tide, there then began a jockeying for position, the *Titanic* being removed from the dock around 10.00am on Saturday 2 March and anchored well clear of the *Olympic* as she was manoeuvred into the dock. The *Titanic* then took the *Olympic's* place at the fitting-out quay as the Thompson Graving Dock was pumped out so that the damage to the *Olympic* could be examined. It took no more than 24 hours to replace the missing propeller blade. But while the laborious process of removing the *Olympic* from the dry dock was underway, and with the *Olympic* being turned so that she was facing the right way to head out to sea and back to Southampton, the ship's hull grounded. Unbelievably, she had to be returned to the dry dock

The *Olympic* and *Titanic* were last seen together in
Belfast in March 1912 when the *Titanic* had to be hauled
out of dry dock and work on her was delayed while the
Olympic was installed in the dry dock to have her port
propeller replaced, having lost it after hitting an unknown
object in the Atlantic 750 miles out of New York.

This was the view looking forward from the rear of the starboard-side second-class promenade area on the boat deck.

for inspection. The whole performance of the manoeuvres and the draining of the dock had to be repeated. In the meantime, the *Titanic* had to wait alongside at the fitting-out quay until her sister ship was given the all-clear and sent on her way.

The *Olympic* finally left for Southampton on 7 March to meet a New York sailing date that had been delayed until 13 March. Work could at last recommence on the *Titanic* to make sure that she was ready for her sea trials and a Board of Trade certification on 1 April. Board of Trade inspectors had, in fact, been reviewing work on the *Titanic* at regular intervals throughout her construction, checking everything from the installation of her four compasses (two on the captain's bridge, one in the platform on the boat deck and one in the stern docking bridge), to the slight camber on her decks designed to aid drainage. The *Titanic's* Marconi radio was installed, connected to its twin aerial wires and tested. The radio could be run either off the main electricity supply from a back-up generator or from a bank of batteries in the radio room. Both broadcast and reception appeared perfect and the *Titanic* was given the call-sign letter MGY.

Among the last items of equipment to be installed were the *Titanic's* lifeboats. The 16 wooden lifeboats were all built by Harland & Wolff. Boats Nos 1 and 2 were emergency cutters, 25 feet (7.6 metres) long and about 7 feet (2 metres) wide with a capacity of 40. The other 14 boats were 30 feet (9 metres) long by approximately 9 feet (2.7 metres) wide and could take 65 passengers. These 16 boats hung from davits supplied by the Welin Davit and Engineering Co. The Welin davits were designed to swing the attached boat out over the side, lower it to the water and then swing back in again for another boat to be attached. At one time, the *Titanic* was intended to have two further boats per davit. Tragically, these were deleted from the final specification.

There were also four Englehardt collapsible boats, which had shallow wooden bottoms and canvas sides – these side 'skirts' could be raised and fastened taut to form a boat that could take up to 47 passengers. Two of these were stowed either side of the officers' quarters and two on the officers' promenade.

In total, the *Titanic* had a lifeboat capacity of 1,178. This was well in excess of Board of Trade regulations, which stipulated that the *Titanic* need have provision for only around 960 lifeboat passengers. These regulations, however, were almost 20 years out of date and were based on the sort of overall passenger capacities of ships three or four times smaller than the *Titanic*. The *Titanic's* 1,178 lifeboat places represented a space for only about one in three of those who would be on board if she was carrying a full complement of passengers and crew. In the end, only 2,207 people would sail for New York – still twice the lifeboat capacity.

Despite the miracle of organisation and planning that went into preparing the *Titanic* for her maiden voyage, there were still some items that would, quite literally, miss the boat. A large bookcase intended for the second-class library arrived too late – delivered to the quayside after the *Titanic* had departed for Southampton. It was sold and then resold, eventually ending up furnishing a civil service office.

While there were some items like the bookcase that were not on board when the *Titanic* left Belfast, there were tradesmen working on the ship who would not have expected to be visiting Southampton. A gang of Harland & Wolff employees, adding final touches, finishing that last lick of paint, would still be hard at work as the *Titanic* headed south and the White Star Line knew that they would be hard pressed to have everything ship-shape in time for the embarkation of passengers. The *Southampton Times and Hampshire Express* reported on this predicament on 30 March, while the *Titanic* was still in Belfast:

The White Star berth will not be vacant very long after the *Olympic's* departure on Wednesday, for the *Titanic* is due to arrive here on the same day. Whatever happens in regard to the coal trouble [a miners' strike was making coal scarce], the White Star Line are as certain as they can be that not only will the *Olympic* get away next Wednesday, but that the *Titanic* will be able to sail on her maiden voyage next week. The *Olympic* has picked up a large quantity of coal in New York, and the *Titanic* is assured of having her bunkers filled. The bookings for both sailings are heavy, and the departure of the two largest ships in the world from the docks within a few days of each other will be an event of considerable interest.

The officials have had so much worry lately that we gladly acceded to their request for our help in making it known that the *Titanic* will not be open for inspection. Already applications have been received from all quarters for permission to visit the ship, and the courteous 'No' has been so often uttered that it was suggested that the services of a gramophone should be requisitioned at once! There is to be no pubic ceremony of any kind. The *Titanic* will enter the Solent without the blare of trumpets or the display of the silver oar. A lot of work will have to be done on board the ship during her week's sojourn at the Docks, and it will be impossible to allow people on board 'except on business'.

The public may not have been allowed on board but, perhaps in return for running the above announcement, a *Southampton Times and Hampshire Express* correspondent was given the opportunity inspect the *Titanic* and was suitably impressed. The following appreciation was printed on 6 April 1912.

In a port where the magnificence of the appointments of the *Olympic* are so well known, it seems scarcely necessary to say much about the *Titanic*. The privileged few who have had the pleasure of visiting the ship since her arrival at Southampton on Thursday morning have been at a loss to express their admiration. One person said that the *Olympic* was all that could be desired, and the *Titanic* was something even beyond that! And if his hearers smiled at his method of putting it, they were to agree that the White Star Line had taken every possible opportunity of effecting improvements, their experience with the *Olympic* having been brought to bear. The *Titanic* had a delightful trip from Belfast to Southampton, and among those on board were Mr Morgan (Morgan,

Grenfell and Co), and representatives of the London and Southampton offices of Café Parisien.

These gentlemen were quick to notice that several changes had been made in the *Titanic*, and particularly was it noticed the increased state room accommodation had been provided. The two private promenade decks were inspected with interest, and they have been instituted in connection with the parlour suite rooms. Then a delightful addition is the Café Parisien, which has been arranged in connection with the restaurant. The deck space outside the restaurant has been utilised for it and it represents an entirely new feature on steamers.

The Café Parisien has the appearance of a charming sunlit verandah tastefully arranged with trelliswork, and chairs in small groups surrounding convenient tables. It will also form a further addition to the restaurant, as lunches and dinners can be served with the same excellent service and all the advantages of the restaurant itself.

In the first-class dining room over 550 passengers can dine at the same time and a feature of the room is the arrangoment of the recessed bays where family and other parties can dine together in semi privacy. The second-class passengers have been very generously provided for. The dining saloon extends the full breadth of the vessel, and will seat 400. The state rooms are of very superior character and the promenades are unusually spacious, a unique feature being the enclosed promenade. The accommodation for third class is also very good, and the vessel will accommodate in all about 3500 passengers and crew.

Although very few of them would have seen this review, everyone in Belfast was justifiably proud of the quality of the workmanship that had gone into the *Titanic*. Indeed, RMS *Titanic* was hailed in some contemporary reports as 'The Pride of Belfast'. The people of Ulster sorely needed such an inspiration, a symbol of hope as growing social and political unrest began to dominate their lives.

This photograph was taken from the tender *America* as she pulled alongside the *Titanic*, which had just anchored off Queenstown. Captain Smith can be seen quite clearly looking down from the highest visible point on the *Titanic*.

PRIDE OF BELFAST

That the people of Belfast took a pride in the *Titanic* and the other ships built at Harland & Wolff is beyond doubt, but not everyone felt quite so warmly about the company itself. A significant proportion had good reason to bear a grudge against the company and this bad feeling has its roots in the sectarianism that has for so long been endemic in the everyday life of the people of Ulster. The Protestant/Catholic religious and political divide affected Harland & Wolff just as it affected every other employer in the province. Harland & Wolff was always seen as a 'Protestant' employer, although the company would always deny that this had ever been official policy. In reality, however, throughout its history only a fraction of the workforce at Harland & Wolff was Catholic. Even in 1992, with most of the modern anti-discrimination laws in place, just five per cent of the workers were Catholic.

There are historical reasons for the imbalance. The shipyard is situated in East Belfast, which was traditionally a Protestant area, and workers were recruited locally. Not only that, but workers were recruited on recommendation. If your father, uncle or cousin worked at the yard, he could vouch for you when a job vacancy arose, and Harland & Wolff, in common with the majority of employers up until recent years, would take the family connection as a strong reference. If the father was a good, reliable worker, then it was assumed that the son would be, too. Furthermore, the strength of family ties meant that new young recruits would work hard and behave well in order not to let down their relatives. Also, the foremen knew well that they could put pressure on the older relatives to keep any youngster showing signs of unruliness on the straight and narrow. Recruiting in this way meant that the skills required in the shipyard stayed within the Protestant community of East Belfast and, as the years went by, little happened to change this.

With the domination of Protestants in the workforce there was very little sectarian disruption within the yard and the minority Catholic element found that most of their colleagues were happy to work alongside them. There was always a small, hard-core element, however, that found it difficult to accept the presence of Catholics and, at times when tension within the community was at its worst, they suffered severe prejudice, a

trend that dragged on into recent times. In 1970, as trouble flared on the streets of Belfast and a spate of shootings erupted, a group of around 100 Harland & Wolff workers scoured some of the workshops, chasing known Catholics off the premises; in 1994 a Catholic worker, Maurice O'Kane, was shot dead at the yard.

During the building of the *Titanic*, when Lord Pirrie was in charge, there was a great deal of unrest among the Protestant workforce about Lord Pirrie's support for Home Rule. The Orange Order was especially concerned about his intentions. Politics and religion for the Protestant majority were largely dominated by the Orangemen, whose history dates back to the roots of sectarian unrest in Ireland.

Irish history is fraught with turbulence, right from the earliest times when the island was made up of a patchwork of small kingdoms whose rulers were constantly battling with each other over land, livestock and longstanding family feuds. Even when the Vikings invaded towards the end of the eighth century, the fearsome Scandinavian warriors who had conquered vast tracts of England and France could not totally subdue the belligerent Irish. They did, however, establish an important permanent trading post, which became Dublin. When the Viking era ended, Dublin retained its significance as a centre of administration and was widely regarded as the island's capital.

Wars between ruling factions in Ireland continued with various kings vying for supremacy until King Dairmait Mac Murchada was driven out of Ireland in the twelfth century. He sought help in England, where he raised an army of Anglo-French noblemen with the blessing of the English king and the Pope in Rome. Thus began the English involvement in Ireland, which became – with Papal approval – a province under English administration, subject to English law and paying English taxes. There then ensued centuries of rebellions and uprisings until, in the middle of the fifteenth century, English influence in Ireland was reduced to an area only about 20 miles (32 kilometres) in extent surrounding Dublin. This area was known as the Pale and was fortified by the English who built a fence around its circumference to keep the Irish out. It is from here that the expression 'beyond the pale' derives.

Above: Lord Charles Beresford, Frederick Smith and founder of the paramilitary Ulster Volunteer Force Edward Carson
head a protest rally against Home Rule at City Hall, Belfast, for the signing of the Covenant on Ulster Day, 1912.

The Pale had its own parliament in Dublin and successfully
extended its authority over the next few years until Henry VIII
took the throne in England. After quelling yet another rebellion,
he made peace with the Irish kings, by now more commonly
known as 'lords', and gained control of most of Ireland. In 1541
Henry rejected the Roman Catholic Church when the Pope
would not grant him permission to marry Anne Boleyn and
installed himself as head of the new Church of England. Irish
churches were ordered to change allegiance to acknowledge
Henry above the Pope, but many refused and Ireland's great
religious divide came into being. Settlers from England and
Scotland were sent to colonise Ireland in order to give
successive English rulers political and religious control over
what was certainly by the time of Queen Elizabeth seen as an
English colony. This resulted in native Irish people being driven
out of their homes, perpetuating the Irish cycle of repression
and violent revolution.

In 1641, just as events in England were about to plunge the
country into civil war, an uprising in Ulster led to the massacre
of up to 15,000 Protestant settlers. Eight years later, the
English King Charles was beheaded and Oliver Cromwell
assumed the title of Lord Protector of the Commonwealth of
England. He had waited a long time to avenge the deaths of
the Ulster Protestants and headed for Dublin with an army of
12,000 men. Bent on revenge and determined to achieve the
suppression of the Irish, Cromwell's troops were given free rein
to commit countless outrages and thousands were slaughtered
in a campaign that lasted a year. Cromwell harboured a bitter
hatred of Catholicism and also expelled around 1,000 Catholic
priests from Ireland during this period, as well as instigating
another of what would today be called 'ethnic cleansing'
programmes – removing Irish from their homes to give their
land and property to his trusted followers.

In 1689, when the English parliament invited the Dutch
nobleman William of Orange to become king in place of King
James II, whose Catholic faith it distrusted, James fled to

The *Titanic* was towed out to commence her sea trials at 6.00am on 2 April 1912. She had been due to undergo the trials the previous day, but high winds had caused a postponement.

Above: Captain Smith with the *Titanic*'s officers. Back row left to right – Chief Purser Hugh McElroy, Sixth Officer James Moody, Third Officer Herbert Pitman, Fifth Officer Harold Lowe, Fourth Officer Joseph Boxhall. Front row left to right – Second Officer Charles Lightoller, Chief Officer Henry Wilde, Captain Smith, First Officer William Murdoch.

France. He decided to stage his comeback via Dublin in 1689 and the decisive battle (with French troops backing James and Danish troops supporting William as part of an ongoing European conflict) took place on the banks of the River Boyne in County Meath in July 1690. Known as the Battle of the Boyne, Protestant settlers from the north fought against Irish Catholics and James's army was routed. The final surrender came in Limerick over a year later, where punitive laws were imposed that reduced Catholics in Ireland to the status of second-class citizens, banning them from basic rights such as taking up professional occupations, owning land or receiving an education.

Over the next 100 years, some civil rights were gradually restored to Catholics. But, alarmed at the way their position of superiority was being eroded, Protestants formed the Orange Order in County Armagh in 1795 in the memory of William of Orange and to demonstrate Protestant loyalty to the British monarchy. As Catholics began to demand equality and even Irish independence from Britain, the Orange Order grew strong on the feelings of insecurity amongst Irish Protestants. More

and more Protestants became involved until the Order, like a Masonic organisation, infiltrated every level of society from the humble labourer to the highest civil servants in the land. Sectarian clashes, and threatened and attempted rebellions rumbled on over the next century. The Orangemen used their July Marches – supposedly in remembrance of the Battle of the Boyne – as an excuse to intimidate Catholics and violence inevitably ensued.

The anti-British feeling among the Irish Catholics was exacerbated by the crop failures of the mid-nineteenth century, which led to widespread famine, a problem that the British Government was not felt to have done enough to alleviate. An Irish Republican Brotherhood, known as the 'Fenians' was formed to bring about an independent Irish state by force. They attempted an uprising in 1867, which was put down by the British, and some politicians in London began to consider that Ireland might better find peace as a self-governing nation.

By the time the *Titanic* was under construction in Belfast, elements of the British government were trying to introduce Home Rule to Ireland, although the Irish Republican Brotherhood had formed a political party that rejected this policy outright, calling for a fully independent Irish nation. When Winston Churchill visited Belfast in 1912 as Lord Pirrie's guest to speak at a meeting of the Ulster Liberal Association, he spoke in favour of Home Rule. Churchill's grandfather, the Earl of Marlborough, had been made Viceroy of Ireland in 1876, and young Winston had moved to Dublin where his father worked as secretary to his grandfather. Winston's father, Lord Randolph Churchill, a conservative MP, had spoken out against previous attempts to bring in Home Rule, coining the phrase 'Ulster will fight – and Ulster will be right' in the knowledge that the Protestant north regarded being ruled from Dublin as totally unacceptable.

'Home Rule Means Rome Rule' was one of the slogans used by Protestant marchers airing their fears that a Dublin parliament would be dominated by Catholics. Thus Lord Pirrie, who chaired the meeting at which Churchill spoke before accompanying him through the town where he was jeered by angry mobs and reportedly pelted with rotten fish as he boarded the steamer to take him back to the mainland, found himself in charge of an organisation that employed thousands of workers who despised his political views.

The religious and political tensions in Belfast and throughout Ireland reached a peak during the First World War, when the Irish Republicans staged a rebellion on Easter Monday 1916 that would eventually lead to the partition of Ireland. The climate on the streets of Belfast while the *Titanic* was taking shape was, therefore, highly volatile. But the community that was seen to be tearing itself apart could justifiably point to the world's largest, most advanced ocean liner and reassure itself as well as the outside world that it was capable of producing more than just a turmoil of bitterness and hatred. The 'Pride of Belfast' may have meant more to some of the city's citizens than others, but the *Titanic* certainly represented a symbol of hope as a marvel of grace and beauty emerging from a country in such terrible conflict.

On 1 April 1912, the *Titanic* was due to undergo her sea trials but high winds forced a postponement until the following day. Even though she left her berth as early as 6.00am a crowd of onlookers gathered to watch her depart. With Captain Smith in command and Board of Trade Inspector Francis Carruthers on board, the *Titanic* headed out into Belfast Lough. Smith's senior officers were Chief Officer Henry Tingle Wilde (39), who

had sailed with Captain Smith on the *Olympic*, First Officer William McMasters Murdoch (41), Second Officer Charles Herbert Lightoller (38), Third Officer Herbert John Pitman (34), Fourth Officer Joseph Groves Boxhall (28), Fifth Officer Harold Godfrey Lowe (28) and Sixth Officer James Paul Moody (34). The captain had a further crew of around three dozen along with almost 80 firemen and trimmers (coal workers) – sufficient manpower to crew the ship for the 12 hours the trials were scheduled to take.

Once out in open water, the *Titanic* commenced a series of manoeuvres, coming up to speed, then stopping, then executing turns at a variety of speeds, while Inspector Carruthers made notes on the performance of the ship and its equipment. A series of snake-like, port-starboard turns to test the *Titanic's* handling were performed, and the engines were run with the port propeller at full astern while the starboard one

Opposite: Francis Browne photographed these passengers boarding the *Titanic* from the tender *America* off Queenstown, Ireland, on the morning of 11 April 1912.

This page: Browne also captured this image of passengers watching the unfolding drama as the *Titanic* left Southampton when her wash caused the liner *New York* to break free from her moorings and be drawn into a near collision.

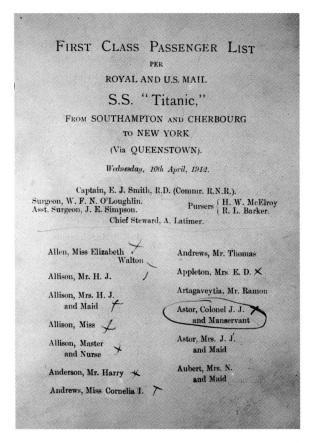

Above: The first sheet of the *Titanic*'s alphabetical listing of first-class passengers. The name of Colonel John Jacob Astor, one of America's richest men, has been circled, perhaps to ensure he receives special attention.

The Marconi operators Jack Phillips (24) and his assistant Harold Bride (22) were also on board, running various tests on the radio equipment and sending and receiving Morse messages (they were not yet equipped with a radio with a speech function) to ensure that the radio worked no matter what the ship was doing. Inspector Carruthers examined everything from the safety equipment and lifeboats, to the water distillation facilities, the operation of the anchors and the certificates of the senior crew members and engineers, before authorising the *Titanic's* passenger certificate and presenting a bill for his services. Other professional fees and expenses amounted to £105 8s 9d.

The *Titanic* was now ready to go into service and was officially handed over by Harland & Wolff to the White Star Line. There was no time for Thomas Andrews and his guarantee group to take time ashore, however, as a quick turnaround was required when the *Titanic* returned to Belfast. She needed the high tide at midnight the next day in order to dock at Southampton, so she left Belfast for good at 8.00pm on 2 April 1912. Her anticipated stop at her home port of Liverpool, where she was to have been opened to the public just as the *Olympic* had been, was cancelled to ensure that she made the tide at Southampton.

Only one incident marred the journey south. A fire was discovered in one of the coal bunkers in No 6 boiler room. This was not an uncommon occurrence on ships of the time and it certainly was not allowed to delay the journey. Several trimmers were assigned to remove the coal from the bunker. The trimmers' regular job, shifting coal manually from one bunker or hold to another to maintain a proper balance or trim throughout a ship's journey as the coal was consumed, was one of the dirtiest and most arduous jobs on the ship. Fighting a fire at the same time was definitely no bonus. The fire stubbornly continued to burn until the bunker was completely emptied of coal, a process that took a full week. Technically, then, not only was the *Titanic* was on fire when she docked at Southampton but also for the whole six days she was berthed there!

There was some concern that a national coal strike might hamper the plans for the *Titanic's* departure as other liners had

was at full ahead before the Inspector was invited to join Captain Smith for lunch in the first-class dining room. An emergency stop was scheduled after lunch, the *Titanic* taking an acceptable 850 yards (777 metres) to come to a halt from 20 knots, before she headed out into the Irish Sea for a 40-mile (64-kilometre) cruise to monitor prolonged straight-line performance.

During this and the return trip, the *Titanic* touched 21 knots for short periods, but was not expected to test her new engines to their full potential until they had been run in service for a while. With good weather, they could expect to achieve her full speed of around 24 knots on her first Atlantic crossing.

been forced to cancel voyages due to severe shortages. Fortunately, the strike ended a few days before she was due to sail and coal was, in any case, transferred from other White Star ships to ensure that the *Titanic* would have enough. By the morning of 10 April 1912, the *Titanic* was fully crewed, fuelled and provisioned – her larder was stocked with enough food to feed an army and included 75,000 pounds (34,000 kilograms) of fresh meat, 25,000 pounds (11,340 kilograms) of poultry and game and 40 tons of potatoes – and she awaited the arrival of her passengers before embarking on her maiden voyage. Strictly speaking, the maiden voyage of a liner was the first trip she made carrying a fare-paying passenger. Since there was reportedly one passenger aboard who had booked from Belfast to New York, as well as a load of mailbags, the *Titanic's* maiden voyage was actually Belfast–Southampton.

At around 9.30am passengers began to appear as the boat-train from London Waterloo arrived to disgorge the first of the 497 third-class and 245 second-class passengers who would board the *Titanic* at Southampton. The 202 first-class passengers arrived on a later first-class train, but all of the passengers and their baggage were on board in time for the *Titanic* to sound her whistles and depart for Cherbourg under the temporary guidance of harbour pilot George Bowyer, bang on time at noon. The ensuing incident with the *New York* when the *Titanic* surged past the smaller, berthed liner causing her to break her moorings and drawing her into a situation that very nearly resulted in a collision, must have been severely embarrassing for George Bowyer. He had also been the pilot on the *Olympic* when she collided with HMS *Hawke*.

Six and a half hours later, the *Titanic* dropped anchor off Cherbourg. The tenders *Nomadic* and *Traffic* delivered some notable first-class passengers, who included the famous fashion designer Lucy, Lady Duff Gordon (whose fashion house 'Lucile' was in London's Hanover Square, just off Regent Street) and her husband, Sir Cosmo Duff Gordon. Also coming aboard was the American mining tycoon Benjamin Guggenheim, whose personal fortune was said to be worth over $50 million. In the first-class dining room that evening they would join the society figures who had embarked at

Southampton. These included Colonel John Jacob Astor IV, reputed to be worth over $85 million, whose real estate empire was said to include a large portion of Manhattan. The 46-year-old entrepreneur had recently divorced and re-married and had left the United States on an extended honeymoon with his second wife, Madeleine, who was just 18. They had been the talk of New York. Now, without doubt, they were the talk of the *Titanic*.

The banker George Widener, whose fortune was estimated at around $30 million, was returning to the United States with his wife and son, while Isador Straus, who owned the New York department store Macy's, was returning from a holiday in Europe with his wife, Ida. Then there was the steel magnate Arthur Ryerson and his wife, the railroad and hotel tycoon Charles M Hays with his wife, Margaret and daughter, Clara, and the special military adviser to the US President, Major Archibald Butt. The *Titanic's* first-class passenger list would have taken up quite a chunk of a US *Who's Who*, one of the major reasons why her sinking caused such a furore in newspaper reports around the world. Nothing makes a newspaper story work better than a liberal sprinkling of references to untold wealth.

Over 140 first-class passengers and 130 second- and third-class passengers joined the *Titanic* at Cherbourg, with 22 passengers, all either first or second class disembarking, having enjoyed an eventful and expensive Channel crossing. The transfer of passengers, baggage and mail took a little over 90 minutes before the *Titanic* was on her way again, headed for Queenstown. The tenders *America* and *Ireland* were waiting for the *Titanic* when she arrived at 11.30am on Saturday 11 April, as were a number of small boats. Enterprising Irish traders had taken to the high seas to try to tempt the *Titanic's* wealthier passengers to buy their wares during the two hours the *Titanic* would be anchored off Queenstown. The tenders brought over 100 third-class passengers, a handful of second-class travellers and 1,385 sacks of mail, which were exchanged for seven first-class passengers who had bought tickets to take them from England to Ireland. Once their business was done, Captain Smith prepared to take the *Titanic* out into the Atlantic.

This page: The *Titanic* bade her last farewell to her native Ireland two hours after she arrived from Cherbourg. As the passengers watched the Irish shoreline fading into the distance, they could not have known that two-thirds of them would never live to see dry land again.

With the Irish coast near Queenstown lying off her bow, the *Titanic* raises her anchors for the last time as she prepares to head out into the Atlantic.

ATLANTIC CROSSING

With the hawkers' small boats pulled well clear, the *Titanic* engaged her mighty engines and headed out into the Atlantic at 1.30pm to the sound of a bagpipe lament played by third-class passenger Eugene Daly who had boarded at Queenstown. Daly may have lamented the fact that he would never see Ireland again, but he was one of the lucky ones who would survive to see America.

Captain Smith took the *Titanic* out into the southern sea lane, long designated as the safest route to take when crossing the Atlantic in all but the warmer summer months. This route should have allowed him to make the crossing avoiding any danger of the freezing temperatures and ice floes found further north. Unfortunately, the late winter and spring of 1912 had been sufficiently mild to cause enormous ice floes to break away from the ice shelf in the far north and drift south.

Each spring many thousands of major icebergs detach themselves from the Arctic ice shelf as the weather warms and the ice retreats northwards. These then slowly melt, continuing to break up into fields of smaller ice the further south they progress. Only a few hundred large icebergs would ever make it as far south as the *Titanic's* route each year, but an unusually high number had been reported by other shipping traffic a week before the *Titanic's* Atlantic voyage. Nevertheless, the *Titanic* was enjoying mild weather and calm seas on the initial leg of her journey, making almost 520 miles (837 kilometres) on her second day out from Queenstown and another 546 miles (879 kilometres) by midday on Sunday 14 April.

Captain Smith's plan was gradually to increase the output from his new engines until – weather permitting – the *Titanic* achieved her top speed. On Sunday, 24 of the 29 boilers were lit and it was expected that the others would be fired up imminently. Although J Bruce Ismay would later strenuously deny that he had issued any instructions to Captain Smith to increase speed, Ismay was certainly aware that this was Smith's intention as the general plan for performance testing had been agreed with all concerned prior to the commencement of the voyage. Charges would be levelled against Ismay that he had urged Smith to abandon caution and 'go for the record' to win the Blue Riband on the *Titanic's* first Atlantic crossing. This was

patent nonsense, especially given Ismay's disdain of the race and the fact that he knew full well that the *Titanic* would never be capable of the matching *Mauretania's* 26 knots.

On Sunday morning the *Titanic's* Marconi operators picked up a message from the Cunard liner *Caronia*, which reported that icebergs, growlers (smaller icebergs) and field ice had been spotted just north of the *Titanic's* intended route. Captain Smith made sure that all of his officers were aware of the report; they would all also have been aware that the tendency would be for this ice to drift south. A further ice warning was received from the Dutch liner *Noordam* later in the morning. In the early afternoon yet another warning came in, this time from the White Star liner *Baltic*. The captain of the *Baltic* reported that a Greek steamer had tracked icebergs and field ice that day in very close proximity to the *Titanic's* position. For some reason, Captain Smith showed this message to J Bruce Ismay, an act that would subsequently be used to sustain the argument that Ismay, not Captain Smith, was running the ship. The message was more likely to have been shown merely for Ismay's information and he certainly felt it of sufficient interest to show it to a number of other passengers before Captain Smith reclaimed it several hours later and had it posted on the bridge for the benefit of his officers.

Shortly after the message from the *Baltic*, the *Titanic* received yet another warning of icebergs in her vicinity, this time from the US Navy's Hydrographic Department, broadcasting to all shipping in the North Atlantic. For some unknown reason this message was never passed from the radio room to Captain Smith. During the course of Sunday afternoon, the outside temperature dropped dramatically and passengers who had previously been able to enjoy sea views from the open decks were forced indoors for the warmth and comfort of the ship's lounges. As night began to fall and the light started to fade, lookouts were specifically instructed to watch for icebergs.

The *Titanic* had six crewmen whose sole jobs were to scan

Opposite: First Officer Murdoch, Chief Officer Wilde, Fifth Officer Lowe and Captain Smith on the deck of the *Titanic*.

the waters ahead of the ship for signs of trouble. They worked in two-man teams in the crow's nest, a small sheltered platform 50 feet (15 metres) up the forward mast. Their shifts lasted two hours, giving them a four-hour break between watches. Normally, given that officers on the bridge would also be watching where they were steering the ship, the two lookouts would have been perfectly adequate. But it was common practice on merchant vessels to post extra lookouts, particularly a forward lookout on the bow, when there was a likelihood of encountering ice. No such lookout was posted aboard the *Titanic*. However, First Officer Murdoch did order that the forecastle hatch should be closed to block light from below and that all forward lights should be extinguished to avoid them interfering with the sight lines from the bridge and the crow's nest.

In the crow's nest itself the two lookouts were annoyed not to have been given binoculars, despite having asked for them in Southampton. Binoculars had been issued to lookouts on the journey from Belfast to Southampton but none were available thereafter. Second Officer Lightoller later admitted that there were several pairs on the bridge and, when questioned at the subsequent inquiry, the lookout Frederick Fleet claimed that with binoculars he could certainly have seen the iceberg sooner. When asked how much sooner, he replied, 'Enough to get out of the way'.

By early evening, as the first of the passengers sat down to dinner in their respective dining rooms, the temperature plummeted to less than four degrees Centigrade and a message was received from the Leyland Line freighter *Californian* – although it was actually intended for the cargo

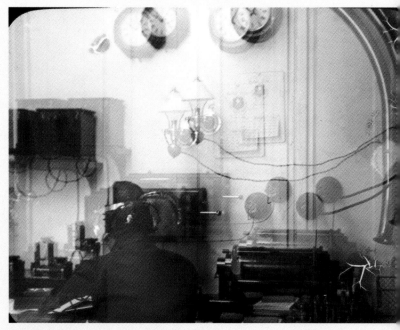

Above: One of Francis Browne's photographs of wireless operator Harold Bride on duty in the radio room listening for signals. Bride and Phillips received numerous Morse messages warning of ice in the *Titanic*'s path, but not all of them were brought to the Captain's attention straight away.

Below: The ice mountain that sealed the *Titanic*'s fate towered at least 75 feet above the surface of the sea, but it was the bulk of ice below the water that did the damage.

ship *Antillian* – advising of several large icebergs in the area. Captain Smith left a party being hosted in his honour by the Philadelphia banker George Widener, his wife Eleanor and their son Harry, around 9.00pm for a situation report from Second Officer Lightoller on the bridge. The temperature was now only a fraction above freezing but it was decided that, following common practice for shipping on this route at that time, they should maintain speed while keeping a sharp watch for ice. The captain retired to his cabin at around 9.30pm.

Ten minutes later, while his subordinate Harold Bride was taking a break, Marconi operator Jack Phillips once again received an ice warning, this time from the Atlantic Transport Lines' *Mesaba*. Phillips, however, was attempting to clear the decks in preparation for his busiest period. Cape Race in Newfoundland was within transmission range and Phillips was determined to deal with sending the backlog of messages from earlier in the day before passengers who had finished dinner

chose to start bombarding him with more requests. Because of reduced interference at night, the Marconi set's range was vastly increased, so it was later in the evening when many passengers (only the wealthier ones, as a 10-word message cost 12s 6d – equivalent today to £150) decided to telegraph friends and relatives to update them on news of the voyage. Having passed on so many ice warnings, Phillips decided to set this one aside – just as he had done with the warning from the US Navy – for delivery to the bridge at a more convenient moment. Perhaps if Phillips had given the message a higher priority, someone on the bridge might have considered it in conjunction with the other warnings – all of which gave positional co-ordinates for the ice sightings – and realised that the *Titanic* was heading straight into a maze of icebergs many miles wide, lying across her path like a frozen mountain range.

But such was the confidence of the *Titanic's* officers in their 'unsinkable' ship and the tried-and-tested practice of trusting to

BILGE KEEL

THE BUCKLED PLATES

FIRST CLASS STATE ROOMS

POST MAIL ROOM

DOUBLE BOTTOM

KEEL

ICE PENETRATING THE DOUBLE BOTTOM

their lookouts that, even if Phillips had delivered the final warning, there is no guarantee that any further steps would have been taken to ensure the safety of the ship. On such a clear night they would surely have expected to spot anything lying in their path. When First Officer Murdoch relieved Second Officer Lightoller at 10.00pm, Lightoller told him that they could expect to see ice at any time. The temperature was now well below zero and Lightoller headed for his quarters and a warm bunk. He was not to rest for long.

In the radio room, Phillips' work was interrupted by a signal from the *Californian* informing the *Titanic* that they were stopped and surrounded by ice but Phillips cut the message short, telling the *Californian* operator not to jam his signal as he was dealing with Cape Race. The operator desisted and listened in for a while longer before calling it a day. The *Californian* had no second operator to take over the monitoring of the radio and was then effectively shut down for the night. Later, as she waited for daylight amid the ice, the *Californian's* lookouts and duty officers would see rockets being fired from an unidentified ship and even attempted to make contact using their Morse lamp, but the ship's master, Stanley Lord, who had

been woken from his sleep, remained unconvinced that the rockets signified anything sinister. Reluctant to try to manoeuvre his ship through the ice, Lord went back to sleep.

Cursing the cold high up in the *Titanic*'s crow's nest, the lookouts Reginald Lee and Frederick Fleet noticed a strange haze on the horizon. A few minutes later at 11.40pm Fleet spotted an iceberg at a distance later estimated to be no more than 500 yards (457 metres) ahead. He immediately sounded three rings on the warning bell in the crow's nest and telephoned the bridge, informing Sixth Officer James Moody that an iceberg lay dead ahead. First Officer Murdoch ordered a turn to port to try to avoid the ice monster and instructed the engine room to give him full speed astern. He also flicked the switch to close the automatic watertight doors down in the bowels of the ship. He knew that with the *Titanic* traveling at over 22 knots, a collision was probably inevitable. Thirty seconds later, the great liner struck the iceberg.

The part of an iceberg that is visible above the surface of the water sits on a mass of ice around eight times bigger. The height of the visible part of the iceberg that Frederick Fleet had spotted looming out of the darkness was estimated at up to 100 feet (30 metres), but it was the massive submerged body of ice that did the damage. Having turned to port, the *Titanic* closed with the iceberg to starboard and the glancing blow that she suffered was enough to slice a 300-foot (90-metre) long incision into the hull below the waterline. The tear in the steel plates was not very wide but it is likely that the impact also popped open some of the riveted joints between the plates. The collision did not cause any unduly worrying bump or crash. Some passengers heard a slight grinding noise, some felt a bit of a shudder, while others sleeping in their cabins noticed nothing at all. Even crew members working in the engine room didn't realise that the *Titanic* had struck something. In No 6 boiler room, however, there was a boom like a clap of thunder and water began pouring in through the slit in the ship's side. With the watertight doors closed, those who could scrambled up the ladder to the deck above to escape the rising torrent.

Captain Smith realised that something was wrong straight away and was on the bridge within a few seconds. Having been

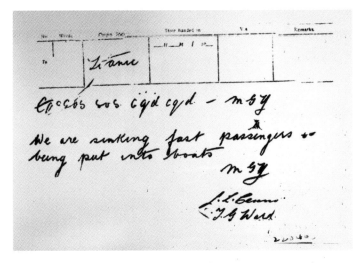

Above: Several ships picked up the *Titanic*'s distress calls, including the *Birma*, whose wireless operators took down this message sent by Jack Phillips who was sending SOS calls as well as the older CQD and the *Titanic*'s call sign MGY.

Opposite: This contemporary illustration shows how the plates buckled when the iceberg struck, although the apparent penetration of the ice into the hull is misleading.

appraised of the situation and assured that the watertight doors were closed, he ordered Fourth Officer Boxhall below for a damage report. The other officers were alerted and hurried to the bridge, as did J Bruce Ismay. Passengers who had lingered after dinner in the lounges chatting or playing cards ventured out on deck and some saw the iceberg drifting away on the starboard side. Some even picked up chunks of ice from the deck as souvenirs. No one thought for a moment that there was any danger of the ship sinking.

Down below on the Orlop Deck, First Officer Boxhall had a different picture. He saw the postal clerks rescuing mailbags from the water flooding into the mail storage room, attempting to manhandle them up to the Post Office on the deck above. He could also see that the water level was rising fast and reported back to Captain Smith. Accompanied by Thomas Andrews, Smith went below to see the damage for himself. Andrews knew in an instant that the *Titanic* was doomed. She had been designed to stay afloat with two of her watertight compartments flooded. The iceberg had slashed open her hull to let water into five compartments. Worse still, the bulkheads separating the compartments did not extend all the way up to the full height of the hull. As water filled the forward compartment it would flood over the bulkhead into the second compartment, and from the second into the third, accelerating the rate at which the compartments flooded and the rate at which she settled at the bows. Andrews estimated that they had no more than two hours before the ship went down.

Ironically, had no evasive action been taken and had the *Titanic* hit the iceberg head on, the damage might have been confined to just one or two compartments, allowing her to stay afloat. Within ten minutes of the accident, there was over 10 feet (3 metres) of water in the first five compartments. Captain Smith now knew that he had no option but to order the evacuation of the ship. He also knew that he could provide only half of those on board with a space in a lifeboat.

There was some confusion among the crew when they were ordered to man the lifeboats. They had had little training with the new davits or their own specific tasks in the case of an emergency such as this. With no public address system to let

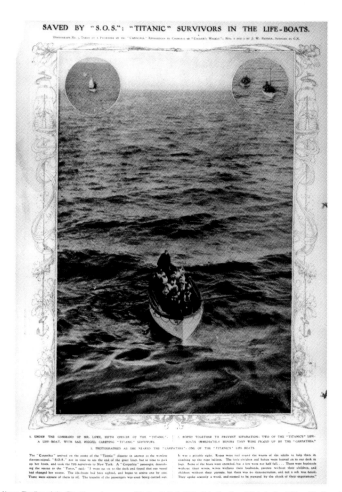

SAVED BY "S.O.S.": "TITANIC" SURVIVORS IN THE LIFE-BOATS.

Above: The first of the *Titanic*'s survivors were picked up in their lifeboats by the *Carpathia* just after 4.00am. The Cunard liner, which had been heading eastward across the Atlantic, then spent five hours bringing survivors aboard and searching for more, before turning back for New York.

the passengers know what had happened they, too, were somewhat confused. Crew members and stewards roused the first- and second-class passengers, helping them on with their lifejackets. When word spread to the third-class areas that the ship was sinking, many clogged the corridors trying to make their way up to the boat deck carrying all of their baggage. Even when they were instructed to leave it behind, some persisted. For the wealthier passengers to leave behind all they were travelling with was one thing, but for many of the immigrants on their way to start a new life, losing their baggage meant losing everything they owned.

Meanwhile, Fourth Officer Boxhall was ordered to make a quick calculation of the *Titanic's* position and Captain Smith gave this to Phillips in the radio room so that he could send out a distress signal. Phillips, with Bride alongside him, sent out the international distress call CQD (often taken to mean 'Come

Quick Danger', although this is not strictly true), as well as the slightly more recent SOS, adopted because of its immediately recognizable Morse pattern and not, as is also often thought, to mean 'Save Our Souls'. Several ships and Cape Race picked up the *Titanic's* distress call but it was the Cunard liner *Carpathia*, heading eastwards bound for the Mediterranean, that emerged as the *Titanic's* best hope of salvation, even though the *Carpathia* was almost 60 miles (96 kilometres) away.

At 12.45am the first of the lifeboats was lowered. Captain Smith had ordered that women and children should go first and the men, mainly first- and second-class passengers at this time, helped the women climb into the lifeboats. Some of the women refused to leave their husbands and many passengers preferred to stay with the mighty *Titanic* rather than take to the ocean in one of the flimsy-looking small boats, refusing to believe that the liner could actually sink. The first boat was lowered less than half full. None of the boats, in fact, left the ship with all of its places taken. The crew were not confident that the boats could be safely lowered when full and they were to take on more passengers from doors that were to be opened in the ship's side closer to the waterline. But the men who were sent to open those doors were never seen again and the doors remained closed.

As the first boat was lowered, distress rockets were fired by Boxhall, who noticed the lights of a ship about 6 miles (10 kilometres) away on the port side. Several of the other officers, including Captain Smith, also saw the lights but the ship could not be contacted by radio or with the use of a Morse lamp. An hour after it was first sighted it seemed to turn away and disappeared.

All of the *Titanic's* boats were lowered and pulled away in time, including two of the Englehardt collapsibles. The other two, lashed to the roof of the officers' quarters, could not be freed in time before the water began washing over the upper decks. Chief Officer Wilde and First Officer Murdoch were attempting to release one of the boats when they were swept to their deaths as the *Titanic* began to go under at around 2.17am. The boat they had been working on was torn clear of its mounting and floated upside down, providing a perilous

sanctuary for around 30 men immediately after the sinking, who balanced precariously on the upturned craft. These included Second Officer Lightoller, washed overboard as the ship went down. He was one of only four of the *Titanic's* officers to survive, the others being Third Officer Pitman, Fourth Officer Boxhall and Fifth Officer Lowe. Captain Smith was reportedly last seen swimming in the sea carrying an infant whom he passed to one of the boats, refusing to come aboard himself in order that he might swim back among the wreckage to help others.

The *Titanic's* 34 engineering officers remained at their posts, keeping the pumps working to try to keep the ship afloat and the lights on for as long as possible. None of them survived. Neither did Thomas Andrews or any of his Harland & Wolff guarantee team. Marconi operator Jack Phillips stayed at his post transmitting the distress call for as long as he could. He went down with the ship. Harold Bride was swept overboard and eventually picked up by one of the lifeboats. None of Wallace Hartley's musicians, who played on deck to calm the passengers until the water began lapping around their feet, survived. Less than a quarter of the *Titanic's* crew of almost 900 were saved. When the 'Pride of Belfast' made her 2-mile (3-kilometre) voyage to the ocean bed, 1,500 of the 2,200 aboard lost their lives.

Many of the most notable of the high society figures aboard were drowned, including Colonel Astor, George and Harry Widener, Major Archie Butt, Arthur Ryerson, Isidor and Ida Straus, and Charles M Hays, but the greatest death toll among the passengers was in third class, with over 440 perishing. Although there were sufficient lifebelts for everyone on board, no one who was left floating in the water could hope to survive in the freezing temperature for very long. By the time the *Carpathia* arrived on the scene at around 4.00am, only those lucky enough to have secured a lifeboat place were left alive. After spending some five hours bringing the survivors aboard and searching for more, the *Carpathia*, which had finally been joined by the *Californian*, left the search to the Leyland Line freighter and set off for New York.

The *Carpathia* arrived in New York at around 9.25pm on

This page: When the news of the disaster broke, crowds of anxious relatives and friends besieged the White Star Line offices in London, Liverpool and on Broadway in New York, desperate for news of loved ones who had sailed on the *Titanic*.

Opposite: Although wireless reports received from the *Carpathia* and other ships in the area were confused, with one report even suggesting that all of the *Titanic*'s passengers and crew had been saved, the grim truth dawned when the *Carpathia* docked in New York.

18 April 1912. A great crowd of anxious relatives and friends, as well as over-eager press reporters, had gathered at the Cunard liner's usual berth, but the *Carpathia* headed instead for the White Star Line pier where she deposited the *Titanic's* lifeboats before finally docking at the Cunard facility.

The United States Senate Inquiry into the sinking of the *Titanic* was launched with seemingly indecent haste at the Waldorf Astoria Hotel in New York on the morning of Friday 19 April. The inquiry was implemented at the instigation of the Michigan Senator William A Smith, a wealthy lawyer and newspaper proprietor who also owned a steamboat company operating around Lake Michigan. Senator Smith had sailed with Captain Smith previously and was determined to discover how a vessel with such an experienced master could come to grief. The number of prominent American citizens aboard the *Titanic* also generated massive interest in the tragedy, perpetuated by sensational headlines in the popular press.

The *Boston Post* estimated that 'the total wealth represented in the first-class passenger list would reach over half a million dollars'. The same newspaper quoted Captain Smith from an interview conducted in 1907:

When he came to New York in command of the *Adriatic* on her maiden trip, he said: 'Shipbuilding is such a perfect art nowadays that absolute disaster, involving the passengers, is inconceivable. Whatever happens, there will be time enough before the vessel sinks to save the lives of every person on board. I will go a bit further. I will say that I cannot imagine any condition that would cause the vessel to founder. Modern shipbuilding has gone beyond that.'

The day before the *Carpathia* docked in New York, as anxious relatives desperate for news of their loved ones formed crowds outside the White Star Line offices on Broadway, Senator Smith presented a resolution before the US Senate in Washington empowering the Committee of Commerce to hold an inquiry. Smith was appointed chairman of the sub-committee investigating the disaster. But, when informed by the US Navy

that they had intercepted signals from J Bruce Ismay stating that he would like to return directly to Britain with the *Titanic's* crew without even setting foot on American soil, he hastily convened the inquiry's first hearings. Senator Smith knew that subpoenas could not be served on foreign nationals compelling them to give evidence to the inquiry if they were not actually in the United States and he wasn't about to let the man he wanted most – J Bruce Ismay – slip through his fingers.

The hearings were to last 18 days and the first witness to be called was J Bruce Ismay. He arrived at the Waldorf Astoria protected by bodyguards after having been portrayed as a despicable villain in the newspapers over the preceding three days for escaping safely from his sinking ship while so many of his passengers drowned. Ismay was the man many regarded as being responsible for the tragedy. He was accused of forcing Captain Smith to order the *Titanic* to sail faster than was safe and of arrogantly demanding a luxurious room aboard the *Carpathia* in order not to share the misery of the other survivors.

Ismay staunchly defended himself against these charges at the hearing both in New York and when the investigation was reconvened in Washington. He maintained that he had boarded the Englehardt collapsible boat 'C' only when there were no women, children or other passengers around and that he was in such a state of distress when he was brought aboard the *Carpathia* that he didn't know what was happening to him. He

Above left: One of the *Titanic*'s lifeboats pulls alongside the *Carpathia*. The photograph has been heavily retouched at the time it was printed and an arrow has been added, apparently pointing to J Bruce Ismay.

Above right: Shocked survivors aboard the *Carpathia*, still scarcely able to believe the horrors they experienced.

ranged over the relationship between White Star and Harland & Wolff then focused on White Star's British parent company, the Oceanic Steam Navigation Company. Ismay answered questions about the value of the company, its stocks and shares, and was finally led by Smith to the IMMC, of which Ismay was President. Establishing who actually owned the *Titanic* was undoubtedly pertinent to the inquiry, but Smith took an inordinate interest in the financial structures of White Star and IMMC. Perhaps he had reasons of his own for wanting to turn the tragedy into a scandal into which he might drag the *Titanic's* ultimate owner, J P Morgan. If that is true, he certainly failed as Morgan's name was never mentioned at the hearings.

J Bruce Ismay did state during the inquiry that, as a result of the disaster, the watertight bulkheads on White Star Line ships would, in future, extend higher to avoid the problem of water flooding over and into the next compartment. He also stated that, 'We have issued orders that none of the ships of our lines shall leave any port carrying more passengers and crew than they have capacity for in the lifeboats.'

The sub-committee's final report was mainly a matter-of-fact appraisal of events leading up to the disaster, the cause of the sinking and a review of those involved. It also recommended that the existing practice of accepting foreign certificates of seaworthiness as being of equivalent merit to the US version be reviewed and that no ship carrying passengers be allowed to leave a US port unless it conformed to US standards. The committee further advised that US standards should be reviewed to ensure that ships were required to have lifeboat places for every passenger and crew member; that ships' radios should be manned 24 hours a day; and that the firing of rockets at sea, except as distress signals, should be made a criminal offence. Among their other comments, they recommended that in future ships should either be built with a double bottom that extended above the full-load waterline to provide a 'second skin', or that longitudinal bulkheads be built to subdivide the watertight compartments. Such bulkheads would be required to continue up to the uppermost continuous structural deck. The area where the report was most scathing was in the conduct of the *Californian* and Captain Lord. It stated that:

was actually given the ship's doctor's quarters.

Senator Smith interrogated Ismay intensely and at length on everything from technical aspects of the ship and the health of Captain Smith, to the speed of the vessel and the £70,000 per year received by the White Star Line from the British Government for transporting the mail. While repeatedly assuring the inquest that he would co-operate fully with the inquiry, provide written affidavits or attend later hearings if required, Ismay submitted a written request for permission to return home to his family on 25 April, also noting that the British Board of Trade was in the process of establishing its own inquiry into the disaster, which would require his presence. Smith dismissed his request, ordering Ismay to remain in the United States and warning him that 'you should continue to help me instead of annoying me and delaying my work by your personal importunities'.

Senator Smith pursued a number of different lines of questioning but was most persistent when attempting to establish the true ownership of the *Titanic*. His questions

The committee was forced to the inevitable conclusion that the *Californian*, controlled by the same company, was nearer the *Titanic* than the 19 miles [30 kilometres] reported by her Captain, and that her officers and crew saw the distress signals of the *Titanic* and failed to respond to them … Had assistance been promptly proffered, or had the wireless operator of the *Californian* remained a few minutes longer at his post on Sunday evening, that ship might have had the proud distinction of rescuing the lives of the passengers and crew of the *Titanic*.

Senator Smith was far more colourful in the address he made to the Senate when presenting the report on what he described as 'the causes leading up to the destruction of the steamship *Titanic*, with its attendant and unparalleled loss of life, so shocking to the people of the world'. While he criticised Captain Lord just as heavily as the written report, he also scolded the British Board of Trade for their 'laxity of regulation and hasty inspection'. But Senator Smith laid the lion's share of the blame for the accident squarely at the door of Captain Smith. While praising the captain's good record and fine character, Smith lambasted him for displaying 'overconfidence and neglect to heed the oft-repeated warnings of his friends', bluntly stating that 'his indifference to danger was one of the direct contributing causes of this unnecessary tragedy'.

The findings of the US inquiry were reviewed by the press on both sides of the Atlantic. Although the official report was generally welcomed by all, Senator Smith's comments and the fact that he bombarded the witnesses with questions in what was seen as an unnecessarily aggressive manner, were roundly condemned. The British *Daily Express* wrote, 'Although much of the report sounds sensible, the grotesque oration of Senator Smith deprives it of much value … Its mock heroics and ludicrous verbosity relieve it of any taint of sincerity or sense'.

The British inquiry into the tragedy was ordered by the Board of Trade and headed by Charles Bigham, Lord Mersey. The Board drew up a list of 26 questions to which it required

Above: J Bruce Ismay faced some stiff questioning about his role in the disaster, but defended himself staunchly both at the hastily-convened Senate Inquiry in New York and at this hearing in Washington DC.

answers from the investigation. These questions ranged from establishing the number of people on board the ship, whether it was adequately designed, manned and equipped, and what precautions were taken when entering the area where ice warnings had been issued, to the details of the accident, the allocation of lifeboat places and the number and status of those saved. Special reference was made to the proportions of first-, second- and third-class passengers saved to determine whether preferential treatment had been given to the more well-heeled passengers. The hearings were opened in the Wreck Commissioner's Court, Royal Scottish Drill Hall, Buckingham Gate, Westminster, on 2 May 1912. The first day was taken up with legal representations and establishing protocol. The first of the 97 witnesses to give evidence, the *Titanic* look-out Archie Jewell, was called on day two.

Jewell was questioned about his recollections of the night of the disaster, setting the scene for the testimonies of those to follow. Among those, on days 11 and 12 of the hearings, was that of Sir Cosmo Duff Gordon. Duff Gordon had been heavily criticised for taking a place in Boat No 1, which had been launched at around 1.10am and was by no means the last of the boats to leave, while there were still so many women on board. Accusations were levelled against him that he had bribed the seamen at the oars of the boat to row away from the area of the wreck after the *Titanic* had gone down. Even though the boat was capable of taking at least 40, only 12 people (including seven crew members) were aboard. They had, therefore, space to take on at least 28 survivors from the water but made no attempt to return for any.

In his testimony to the inquiry, Leading Fireman Charles Hendrickson, one of the crew members ordered to man Boat No 1, claimed that they had obeyed the orders they had been given when the boat was launched and had pulled away from the *Titanic* for 200 yards (182 metres) before stopping to wait for further orders or to be recalled. When the ship went down he claimed the cries of those in the water were clearly audible, yet when he suggested that they return to pick up survivors, Sir Cosmo and Lady Duff Gordon had objected because 'they were scared to go back for fear of being swamped'. It had been claimed that Duff Gordon had offered each of the seamen £5 to ignore the cries for help as the panicking passengers in the water would capsize the boat when too many of them attempted to climb aboard.

Duff Gordon strenuously rebutted all of these accusations, denying ever having heard any discussion in the boat about turning back to pick up survivors and maintaining that the money he had given to the men had been to help them replace their lost kit. He had been told during a conversation with one of the men in the boat that the White Star Line would stop their pay from the moment the ship sank and that they would receive no compensation for their loss. His gift of £5 to each man was made out of compassion and not as any sort of bribe. The money was duly handed over when the boat's occupants were picked up by the *Carpathia*. But, whatever the circumstances surrounding the payment, the fact that Duff Gordon had boarded a boat while other distinguished gentlemen had stayed behind and had not returned to rescue other survivors scarred him with a dishonour that would shame him for the rest of his days.

Following his experience at the hands of Senator Smith in America, J Bruce Ismay took the stand in Westminster on days 16 and 17 of the British inquiry, well prepared for a repeat of his ordeals in New York and Washington. He faced the same sort of questions with which Senator Smith had confronted him and answered them in much the same fashion, fully aware that Lord Mersey's team had transcripts of all of the Senate Inquiry's witness statements to which they could refer. The Wreck Commissioner's Inquiry, however, seemed less intent on pinning the blame for the sinking of the *Titanic* on Ismay. When his report was finally published on 30 July 1912, Lord Mersey stated that there had been:

the suggestion that, as Managing Director of the Steamship Company, some moral duty was imposed upon him to wait on board until the vessel foundered. I do not agree. Mr Ismay, after rendering assistance to many passengers, found 'C' collapsible, the last boat on the starboard side, actually being lowered. No other people were there at the time. There was room for him and he jumped in. Had he not jumped in he would merely have added one more life, namely his own, to the number of those lost.

Lord Mersey was less kind about Sir Cosmo Duff Gordon:

I have said that the members of the crew in that boat might have made some attempt to save the people in the water, and that such an attempt would probably have been successful; but I do not believe that the men were deterred from making the attempt by any act of Sir Cosmo Duff Gordon's. At the same time I think that if he had encouraged the men to return to the position where the *Titanic* had foundered they would probably have made an effort to do so and could have saved some lives.

Following the sinking of the *Titanic*, many alterations were made to the *Olympic* in the light of the lessons learned from her sister ship's design flaws. The third of the Olympic-class liners, the *Gigantic*, incorporated the redesigned bulkhead and watertight compartment designs during her construction two years later. She was renamed the *Britannic* in an effort to break the link with the *Titanic*.

AFTERMATH

Having considered all of the evidence, the Wreck Commissioner's Inquiry found that the *Titanic* was lost 'due to collision with an iceberg, brought about by the excessive speed at which the ship was being navigated'. Just as the US report had done, Lord Mersey laid most of the blame for the unnecessary loss of life during the disaster at the feet of Captain Lord and the crew of the *Californian*. The captain and the relevant members of his crew were questioned at length; ultimately Lord Mersey surmised that:

> The vessels were about five miles [eight kilometres] apart at the time of the disaster. The evidence from the *Titanic* corroborates this estimate, but I am advised that the distance was probably greater, though not more than eight to ten miles [twelve to sixteen kilometres]. The ice by which the *Californian* was surrounded was loose ice extending for a distance of not more than two or three miles [three or four kilometres] in the direction of the *Titanic*. The night was clear and the sea was smooth. When she first saw the rockets the *Californian* could have pushed through the ice to the open water without any serious risk and so have come to the assistance of the *Titanic*. Had she done so she might have saved many if not all of the lives that were lost.

Again in accordance with Senator Smith's findings, Lord Mersey recommended that ships should be built with watertight compartments that were divided longitudinally and extended up to the highest main deck. Such designs should be created in conjunction with a double bottom that extended above the waterline. He further recommended that the Board of Trade be given immediate powers to enforce such regulations. As far as lifeboats were concerned, Lord Mersey called for a lifeboat space for every person on board every ship and insisted that drills should be held more regularly.

He did not find that the third-class passengers had been deliberately neglected at the expense of the first and second classes, but he did criticise the organisation on the *Titanic* of the procedures for manning the lifeboats. The report stated that

there was no evidence to suggest that 'the third class passengers had been unfairly treated; that their access to the Boat Deck had been impeded, and that when at last they reached that deck the first- and second-class passengers were given precedence in getting places in the boats'.

Nevertheless, only 38 per cent of the third-class passengers were saved, compared with over 60 per cent of first class and more than 40 per cent of second class. Lord Mersey stated that the greater proportion of first- and second-class passengers saved could be accounted for 'by the greater reluctance of the third class passengers to leave the ship, by their unwillingness to part with their baggage, by the difficulty in getting them up from their quarters, which were at the extreme ends of the ship, and by other similar causes'. This, along with the statement of Mr Harbinson who attended the inquiry to represent the interests of relatives of some of the third-class passengers who died, has led to the report being slated as a whitewash. Harbinson declared that 'no evidence has been given in the course of this case which would substantiate a charge that any attempt was made to keep back the third-class passengers'.

The whitewash accusations also extended to Lord Mersey's appraisal of the conduct of Captain Smith leading up to the disaster. Although the report stated quite clearly that the collision with the iceberg was 'brought about by the excessive speed', Lord Mersey accepted, on the evidence given by captains of other ships, that 'for a quarter of a century or more the practice of liners using this track when in the vicinity of ice at night had been in clear weather to keep the course, to maintain the speed and to trust to a sharp look-out to enable them to avoid the danger'. This policy had not in the past resulted in any major accidents or loss of life and Lord Mersey sympathised with Captain Smith who 'had not the experience which his own misfortune has afforded to those whom he has left behind'. In Lord Mersey's opinion, having received warnings of ice but decided not to slow the ship or post extra look-outs, Captain Smith had:

> made a mistake, a very grievous one, but one in which, in face of the practice and of past experience, negligence

cannot be said to have had any part; and in the absence of negligence it is, in my opinion, impossible to fix Captain Smith with blame. It is, however, to be hoped that the last has been heard of the practice and that for the future it will be abandoned for what we now know to be more prudent and wiser measures. What was a mistake in the case of the *Titanic* would without doubt be negligence in any similar case in the future.

Captain Smith was, therefore, exonerated by Lord Mersey, his reputation saved. The same could not be said for Captain Lord. Following the controversy created by the US and British inquiries, Lord was forced to resign from the Leyland Line. He then joined a London freight line, the Nitrate Producers Steam Ship Company, as a ship's captain, and remained with that company until his retirement in 1927. Lord fought to clear his name in the aftermath of the inquiries, insisting that the

Californian was further away and that she was not the ship seen by those on board the *Titanic*. Although he finally decided to try to put it all behind him, each new film released or book published about the disaster where he was inevitably painted as the villain of the piece, caused him great distress.

When the 1958 movie *A Night to Remember* was released, Lord made one last attempt to salvage his good name and it finally emerged that there may have been another vessel in the area that had not previously been taken into consideration. A Norwegian vessel had been illegally hunting seals in Canada and had been heading home via the route where the *Titanic* struck the iceberg. The Norwegians had no radio and took the distress rockets to be a Canadian government vessel signalling them to stop. They didn't. Even if the mystery Norwegian ship was the one seen by the *Titanic*, it doesn't excuse the *Californian* having failed to act on seeing the distress rockets.

Stanley Lord died in 1962 but the debate about the

Left: The man appointed by the British Board of Trade to lead the official Wreck Commissioner's Inquiry into the *Titanic* tragedy was Lord Mersey, seen here with his son. The British hearings opened in Westminster, London, on 2 May 1912.

Californian raged on, especially when the wreck of the *Titanic* was discovered by a team from the Woods Hole Oceanographic Institute of Massachusetts in September 1985 – 13 miles (21 kilometres) from the position given in her distress signals. The truth about the position of the *Californian* in relation to the *Titanic* on the night of 14 April 1912 may never be known.

Although the *Titanic*'s surviving officers – once seen as the cream of the White Star Line – were not castigated in the same way as Captain Lord, their careers never recovered from the association with the disaster. None of the four ranking officers was ever to be given command of his own vessel. Second Officer Charles Herbert Lightoller served with the Royal Navy during the First World War, after which he became Chief Officer of the White Star Line's *Celtic*. When it became clear that his seafaring career stood little chance of progressing much further, he retired – not yet 50 years of age and with 30 years of experience at sea. He ran a chicken farm and kept a yacht called the *Sundowner*, which he sailed across the English Channel in 1940 as part of the makeshift evacuation fleet called upon to rescue Allied troops from the beaches of Dunkirk.

Third Officer Herbert John Pitman persevered with his naval career through both the First and Second World Wars and was awarded an MBE in 1946 for his unstinting service to Britain's Merchant Navy. Fourth Officer Joseph Boxhall had two notable reunions with the *Titanic*, although the first was on Ruislip Reservoir. The reservoir, close to Pinewood Studios, was used to shoot some of the scenes during the making of the 1958 movie *A Night to Remember*, on which Boxhall was employed as a technical adviser. Joseph Boxhall's second encounter with the great ship was in 1967 when his ashes were scattered in the Atlantic over the spot where the *Titanic* came to grief.

Fifth Officer Harold Lowe, who had fired the warning shots to stop panicking third-class passengers storming the lifeboats, became Third Officer on the White Star Line's *Medic*, one of the company's 'Jubilee' class providing a regular service between Britain and Australia. At just 12,000 tons, the *Medic* was a fraction of the *Titanic*'s size, could accommodate only 320 passengers and made a mere 13.5 knots, although she could carry a substantial load of freight. No one, however, would have regarded Lowe's posting to the *Medic* as a promotion. During the First World War, Lowe served in the Royal Navy and afterwards decided to retire from the sea.

The men involved in the building of the *Titanic* emerged from the catastrophe faring far better than her surviving officers. J Bruce Ismay returned home to Liverpool where he was greeted as a hero, several women having testified to Lord Mersey's inquiry that they owed their lives to Ismay having ushered them into lifeboats. Although vilified by the American press, a statement he gave to *The Times* and the support he received from Lord Mersey stood Ismay in good stead at home. Nevertheless, he was often said to be a 'broken man' who had been forced into retirement just over a year after the sinking of the *Titanic*. In fact, Ismay had been planning his retirement from IMMC and the White Star Line for some time prior to the accident. He had numerous other business interests, which he maintained up until around 1920 when he sold Sandheys. He then divided his time between his London home and a country house, Costelloe Lodge in County Galway, where he fished for salmon in the Casla River that flowed through the grounds. He was said to have caught over 300 salmon there in one season.

When Costelloe Lodge was destroyed by fire, Ismay oversaw the rebuilding programme and continued to enjoy family holidays there with his wife, Florence, their children and grandchildren. In 1936, circulatory disease forced the amputation of his right leg and his health continued to deteriorate until he died of a stroke in October 1937 at the age of 74. Florence Ismay, who had become a British subject after her marriage, spent many years following the death of her husband visiting her children, grandchildren and relatives in England and America. In 1949 she took an Oath of Repatriation to become an American citizen once more, although she spent her final days in England, where she died in 1963.

J Bruce Ismay's ultimate boss, J P Morgan, was in Europe when the *Titanic* was due to set sail for New York and was expected to return to the United States aboard the pride of IMMC's fleets. He had a suite booked, suite B52, supposedly designed to his own taste, which was the accommodation that

Above: One of the *Titanic*'s four surviving officers, Third
Officer Boxhall, was employed as a technical adviser on
the 1958 movie *A Night To Remember*.

would be reserved for him whenever he crossed the Atlantic. Morgan did not, however, join the ship for the journey as the 75-year-old tycoon claimed that he was too ill to travel. Suite B52 was occupied by Ismay along with his valet, John Fry, and his secretary, William Harrison, neither of whom were as fortunate as their employer when the *Titanic* foundered. Both were drowned. J P Morgan may well have felt too poorly to contemplate the transatlantic voyage, but two days after the *Titanic* sank, a newspaper reporter managed to track him down to the French health resort of Aix-les-Bains, where Morgan was staying at the spa town's Grand Hotel in the company of his French mistress.

J P Morgan had weathered many financial storms and economic disasters throughout his chequered career, but the *Titanic* tragedy was believed by some to have affected him more deeply than many might have expected. Financially, the

loss of the *Titanic* and the subsequent compensation claims were a huge, but not terminal, setback to his plans for a North Atlantic monopoly. The political situation in Europe as the continent slid inexorably towards war played a far bigger role in scuppering his price-fixing schemes. In any case some, although by no means all, of the monetary losses were covered by insurance.

The loss of prestige in the face of the competition, however, could never be fully recovered. But more even than that, the deaths of 1,500 passengers were said to have weighed heavily on the old man. Perhaps this was because he believed those passengers had trusted him, through his shipping conglomerate, to carry them safely across the ocean and J P Morgan was a man who placed a great deal of value in trust. He once told a US congressional committee that capital and assets were not what mattered most to him as a banker when considering offering credit. The thing that mattered most was the character of the applicant: 'A man I do not trust could not get money from me on all the bonds in Christendom'. J P Morgan died aged 76, a year after the sinking of the *Titanic*.

Another VIP scheduled to sail on the *Titanic's* first Atlantic crossing, who also cancelled because of illness, was one of the masterminds behind the building of the ship – Lord Pirrie. Following the sinking of the *Titanic*, Lord Pirrie remained in charge at Harland & Wolff as the *Olympic* returned to the yard for modifications to her bulkheads, to have her double bottom extended and to be equipped with new lifeboats. Politically, Pirrie had a rough ride in Belfast in 1912 because of his support for Home Rule but, on the business front, Harland & Wolff went from strength to strength under his guidance. They bought another shipyard at Govan on the Clyde and, when the First World War broke out in 1914, Lord Pirrie's energy and

Far left: Two years after the sinking of the *Titanic*, the First World War broke out and the Harland & Wolff yard was busier than ever. Here the light cruiser *Vindictive* is launched from *Olympic's* No 2 slipway.

Left: Harland & Wolff's shipbuilding programme during the Second World War made them a prime target for Germany's Luftwaffe and in May 1941 almost half of the yard was destroyed in bombing raids.

talents in shipbuilding were utilised to the full in service of his country.

Pirrie was happy to be called upon to devote all of Harland & Wolff's resources to helping the war effort. He oversaw the conversion of 14 merchant ships into armed cruisers before launching into a massive warship construction programme. Ten gunships were built before the company began work on the light cruisers *Glorious* and *Vindictive*, which were modified during construction to carry aircraft. Lord Pirrie even established an aircraft manufacturing plant where Harland & Wolff constructed the Avro 504 fighter bomber. He was made Comptroller-General of Merchant Shipping and laid out a whole new yard to mass-produce 'standard' ships to identical design quickly and cheaply in order to replace vessels lost during the conflict. In 1917 Harland & Wolff built five 'standard' ships and within a year had built a further eleven with 23 more on order.

In 1921 Lord Pirrie became a Viscount and was one of the first senators elected to the new parliament in Northern Ireland in 1922. He was also made a Knight of St Patrick, a member of the Privy Councils of both Ireland and England, Chancellor of Belfast's Queen's University and High Sheriff of County Antrim and County Down, among many other honours. In 1924 Viscount Pirrie, accompanied by the Viscountess, embarked on a tour of ports in Brazil, Uruguay, Argentina, Chile, Peru and Ecuador to study shipping prospects for the Pacific Steam Navigation Company, of which he was a stockholder. On his way to New York on the PSNC's liner *Ebro*, the 77-year-old Viscount died of bronchial pneumonia.

Viscount Pirrie's brother-in-law, Alexander Carlisle, did not sail on the liner he had played such a prominent part in creating, but this was not entirely through his own choice. He travelled from his London home to Southampton to watch *Titanic's* departure and was reportedly asked why he was not on board, replying that he had not been invited. Carlisle was married with three children and, after his retirement from Harland & Wolff, he became something of an eccentric figure, collecting autographs and riding a bicycle around London before it had become even remotely fashionable. He also swam every day, whatever the weather, in the Serpentine in Hyde Park. A year after the death of his brother-in-law, Alexander Carlisle, aged 71, died after catching a severe chill.

The company to which both men had devoted so much of their lives and whose workforce produced the *Titanic* grew ever more powerful as the years progressed. The Musgrave Yard founded by Lord Pirrie became the focus of Harland & Wolff's output, playing as vital a role in the company's efforts during the Second World War as it had during the First. Over the 30 years or so that encompassed the two wars and the inter-war period, Harland & Wolff produced almost 140 ships for the British Navy, including six aircraft carriers. One of the ships built for the navy was the cruiser HMS *Belfast*, named after the city in which she was built. HMS *Belfast* was launched on St Patrick's Day, 17 March 1938, and commissioned into the Royal Navy just one month before the Second World War began in 1939. She was soon in action but struck a mine while leaving the Firth of Forth in November 1939 and spent three years under repair. When she re-entered the war, the *Belfast* was one of the most modern and powerful ships in the Royal Navy. She escorted Arctic convoys and had the honour of firing some of the first shots during the bombardments in support of the D-Day landings. HMS *Belfast* also served in Korea. After she retired, she was eventually brought to London in 1971 where she now rests as a floating museum on the Thames in the shadow of Tower Bridge.

During that same 30-year period, Harland & Wolff also built around 130 merchant vessels and their prolific output was a source of great irritation to the Germans. The Luftwaffe bombed the yards in April and May of 1941, destroying over half of the facilities, but within two years Harland & Wolff was back to full production once again. After the Second World War, the Belfast shipyard continued to build some of the largest and most advanced ships in the world, including the aircraft carrier HMS *Eagle* and, in 1960, the luxury liner *Canberra*, the largest passenger ship to be built since the end of the Second World War. *Canberra* herself saw military service when she carried troops to the Falklands in 1982.

Constantly evolving in order to stay at the forefront of the shipbuilding industry, Harland & Wolff reorganised the

Musgrave Yard in the early 1960s – doing much as Lord Pirrie had done over half a century before when preparing to build the Olympic-class liners – and converted six slipways into five larger ones to build ever bigger ships. They built Britain's first supertanker, the 190,000 ton *Myrina*, in 1969 and later developed a new process, prefabricating whole sections of a ship to be joined together rather than building the hull plate by plate.

Despite all the efforts of the company, which continued to demonstrate its technical prowess building highly advanced ships for the oil industry throughout the 1970s, 80s and 90s, Harland & Wolff became a symbol of Britain's industrial decay. It lost out on much-needed shipbuilding orders to foreign competition – most notably from the Far East – to such an extent that by 1975 the company was facing closure. Appalled at the prospect of thousands of Belfast workers losing their jobs, the British Government nationalised the yard and spent billions in subsidies trying to keep the business afloat. After almost 15 years of gradual decline, Harland & Wolff was bought back from the government by its own management and employees in partnership with the Norwegian shipping tycoon Fred Olsen. Sadly, it became impossible to maintain the company as a ship builder. The last ship to be constructed at Harland & Wolff was the ferry *Anvil Point* in 2003, on completion of which all but 130 of the workforce was made redundant.

The Belfast yard had at one time employed around 35,000 people. Harland & Wolff still exists, with regular contracts for the repair and maintenance of all kinds of vessels as well as providing a design and technical consultancy to ship builders and the oil industry. They have even built bridges, ironic since they once employed a bridge builder to produce the gantry cranes required for the construction of the *Titanic* and *Olympic*.

RMS *Olympic* was soon back in service on the transatlantic run with her modifications and extra lifeboats in place. She continued to cross the Atlantic even after the First World War broke out, but the passenger trade dropped off quite substantially when the U-boat menace made people realise that travelling thousands of miles in such a tempting target

In 1915, when the *Olympic* was commissioned into the Royal Navy as HMT (His Majesty's Transport) *Olympic* to ferry service personnel to and from the Aegean, she was given a bizarre 'dazzle' camouflage paint scheme. This was intended to break up her outline, making it harder for German submarine crew to identify her through their periscopes and hopefully harder for them to fix an accurate range before launching their torpedoes.

might not be such a good idea.

In October 1914, the *Olympic* was ordered back to Belfast where, once she had disembarked her passengers at Southampton, the White Star Line intended to mothball her until the war was over. On her way to Southampton, the *Olympic* rescued the entire crew of HMS *Audacious,* which had been crippled by a German mine, and took the warship in tow, although the tow lines parted in heavy seas and the *Audacious* had to be abandoned, her magazines later exploding and sealing her fate. Only six months later, *Olympic* was commissioned into the Royal Navy as a troop transport and HMT (His Majesty's Transport) *Olympic* sailed for Greece resplendent in a bizarre multi-coloured camouflage scheme. The bold stripes and geometric shapes were intended to confuse enemy range-finders, but had the effect of making the once-graceful *Olympic* look like a graffiti victim.

With much of her luxurious interior stripped bare, the *Olympic* could carry up to 7,000 troops and was armed, following a further visit to Belfast in 1917, with anti-submarine guns. In 1918, the *Olympic* actually accounted for a German submarine, which she first shelled and then rammed, sinking it almost instantly – the only victory for any merchant ship against any German warship during the entire course of the war. The American servicemen the *Olympic* was carrying at the time donated money from an impromptu collection to have a plaque made for display aboard the *Olympic* in honour of this achievement. The *Olympic* ended the war carrying Canadian troops home before returning to Harland & Wolff to be refitted for regular passenger service again. While she was being examined in Belfast, workers discovered a large dent in the *Olympic's* hull, thought to have been caused by a German torpedo that, unknown to anyone, had struck the ship but malfunctioned, failing to explode.

With her luxurious interior refitted and refurbished, the *Olympic* returned to cross the Atlantic under the flag of the White Star Line, having been converted to burn oil instead of coal. She suffered one desperately unfortunate incident in May 1934 when, approaching New York in heavy fog, the *Olympic* rammed and sank the Nantucket lightship. Seven of the

lightship's crew were killed in the incident. The following year the *Olympic* was retired and, with no prospect of finding a buyer for the ageing liner who might be willing to operate her as a working vessel, she was sold for scrap. The *Olympic's* final voyage under her own steam was to Jarrow on the River Tyne, where she was stripped bare before her hull was towed to Inverkeithing on the Firth of Forth to be dismantled.

On Tyneside, her fittings were auctioned off and much of her interior was bought by Douglas Smith, a director of the Smith and Walton paint factory, for £800. Smith and Walton's office complex was subsequently decorated with arched window frames from the *Olympic's* gymnasium. The stateroom doors were used throughout the building, which also incorporated corridors of carved oak panelling from the main second-class staircase and the carved wooden entrance and doors to the second-class dining room. Smith and Walton's employees enjoyed eating in a canteen fitted with carved wood from the *Olympic's* first-class smoking room, illuminated by lights from first-class passageways. Even the canteen toilets came from the *Olympic.*

There were intended to be three Olympic-class sister ships and work began on the third ship, the *Gigantic,* on 30 November 1911. Her keel was laid on Slipway No 1 where the *Olympic's* construction had begun. When the *Titanic* was sunk five months later, work on the new ship was halted. In the light of the findings of both the US and UK inquiries, as well as Harland & Wolff's and the White Star Line's own consideration of the causes of the disaster, it was clear that a major redesign was required. The epic name, intended to be the most inspiring of the trio – *Olympic, Titanic* and *Gigantic* – was also changed to the less imposing *Britannic.*

The work on new bulkheads and a double skin as well as other improvements, made the *Britannic* the largest of the three sister ships at almost 50,000 tons. She had new lifeboat davits capable of handling six boats, although not all of the davits were of the new type when the *Britannic* left the yard in a hurry in December 1915. Launched in February 1914, it was expected that the *Britannic* would enter transatlantic service in early 1915. The outbreak of the First World War in the summer of

1914 put paid, not only to the plans for the *Britannic's* maiden voyage, but also to her completion. Workers and materials were required for the war effort and the luxury liner had to take second place.

Eventually, the *Britannic* was called up for duty as a hospital ship and her interiors were finished with hospital bunks and treatment rooms rather than opulent suites, smoking rooms, libraries and dining salons. She was painted white with a green stripe along her hull and red crosses to let the enemy know that this was a non-combatant ship. The *Britannic* left Belfast for Liverpool then, just before Christmas 1915, having embarked her crew and medical staff, she set out on her maiden voyage to the Greek island of Lemnos via Naples. On Lemnos, HMHS (His Majesty's Hospital Ship) *Britannic* took on casualties from the battles in the Dardanelles and headed for Southampton, where she docked in January 1916. Within a fortnight she was headed back to Naples where her orders were to bring casualties from other, smaller hospital ships back to the UK. After another similar trip, the *Britannic* spent a couple of months

Above: During the First World War, Lord Pirrie established an aircraft manufacturing plant at Harland & Wolff where the company produced the Avro 504 fighter bomber.

idle before being released by the Admiralty in June 1916 as they considered that they had no more use for her. The *Britannic* headed back to Belfast to be completed to the White Star Line's requirements, but within two months the small port of Mudros on Lemnos had once again become a casualty clearing station and the *Britannic* was pressed into service once more.

The *Britannic's* shuttle service between Southampton and the Aegean continued until 21 November 1916 when, having left Naples at around 8.00am, a massive explosion on the starboard bow erupted as she negotiated the Kea Channel. It is unclear whether she struck a mine or was torpedoed. It has been speculated that the Germans believed the medical supplies she was carrying were actually munitions and that made her a legitimate target. Thirty people died needlessly when the lifeboats they were in were lowered while the ship was still moving and were sucked into the propellers, there to be smashed to pieces. The remainder of the passengers and crew escaped in lifeboats (the *Britannic* had 58) once the ship had been brought to a halt. The *Britannic* then sank 400 feet (122 metres) to the seabed, a shallow grave for such a grand ship. When her bow touched the bottom, her stern would still have been well above the surface.

The two ships that most inspired the building of the *Titanic*, the *Lusitania* and *Mauretania*, suffered fates strangely similar to their White Star rivals the *Titanic* and *Olympic*. Like the *Olympic*, the *Mauretania* was requisitioned by the Admiralty for use as a troop transport during the First World War. Also like the *Olympic*, she was painted in a chequerboard of dazzle camouflage and sailed to the same ports as the *Britannic*, delivering and evacuating troops from Gallipoli and the Dardanelles campaign. In May 1919 she was released from wartime service and returned to England to be refitted as a luxury liner, but the refit did not include a complete overhaul of her turbines. Consequently, the *Mauretania's* Atlantic crossing speeds were greatly reduced as wartime service had left her engines badly in need of a major overhaul.

In July 1921, by which time she was struggling to achieve 20 knots, a fire broke out, destroying much of the first-class accommodation and first-class dining room. The *Mauretania* returned to the Tyneside yard of Swan, Hunter and Wigham Richardson, where she had been built, to undergo repairs. At the same time, her turbines were overhauled and the boilers converted to burn oil rather than coal. The six-month repair programme included extensive modernisation of the furnishing and fittings and, when she returned to service in March 1922, she was once again among the fastest and most luxurious passenger liners in the world. She achieved over 27 knots on one trip and broke her own record for the Atlantic Crossing in both directions, but she was not quite fast enough to compete with the new German liner *Bremen*, which could make almost 29 knots and claimed the Blue Riband in 1929. The *Mauretania* made her last Atlantic crossing in September 1934. Stripped of her luxury furnishings, she made her final journey from Southampton to the breakers' yard at Rosyth in July 1935 where, again like the *Olympic*, the ageing liner ended her life.

The *Lusitania's* career was, sadly, rather more like that of the *Titanic* in the way that it ended. She continued to operate as a passenger ship on the Atlantic route following the outbreak of the First World War until, on 7 May 1915, she was torpedoed by a German submarine off the southern coast of Ireland. The explosion was said to have sounded like a gigantic rumble of thunder and was followed shortly afterwards by a second blast, the source of which has become a point of great contention. This second explosion may have been caused by cold sea water rushing in and engulfing the boilers, which would then have exploded, or it may have been a second torpedo.

One other explanation is that, as well as carrying civilian passengers, the *Lusitania* had in her holds a consignment of artillery shells and millions of rounds of small arms ammunition disguised as boxes of cheese and other regular cargo. Supplying such military aid would have contravened the laws of the then neutral United States and made the liner a perfectly legitimate target for the Germans. Whatever caused the second explosion, the *Lusitania* was doomed. Although 764 were rescued, 1,200 passengers, many of them American citizens, lost their lives in the tragedy. The outrage caused by the attack hastened America's entry into the First World War.

Although the loss of the *Titanic* might have been expected to cripple the White Star Line, the company remained in strong competition on the Atlantic route, despite the compensation claims and the publicity attracted by the huge sums involved. White Star paid out almost £3.5 million in compensation for the loss of life and property on the *Titanic*, the highest payment being made to Charlotte Drake Cardeza whose list of lost belongings extended to over a dozen pages and amounted to £36,567. Despite all of this, White Star claimed a respectable percentage of the 2.6 million passengers who crossed the Atlantic in 1913. They carried over 191,000 passengers, which compared favourably with Cunard's total of almost 200,000. The German company Hapag, however, easily trumped their achievements with almost 250,000 passengers as the tide of US immigrants continued to flow most strongly from Germany and eastern Europe.

That was all to change the following year with the outbreak of war. From 1914 to 1918 much of the White Star fleet was either on military service or laid up for the duration of the war. The lack of passengers made maintaining a regular viable transatlantic service extremely difficult. Added to this there was a shortage of coal as so much was being consumed by the Royal Navy, and a lack of firemen, trimmers and other crew to man the ships as so many men were called up. White Star managed to keep their passenger service running throughout the war years, except in 1917, but with a greatly reduced number of journeys.

After the war, business picked up and White Star was once again the jewel in IMMC's crown – for a while. In the 1920s the American Depression severely affected the North Atlantic passenger trade. There were fewer immigrants, fewer wealthy tourists heading for Europe and new US legislation designed to protect its merchant fleets. As White Star Line ships sailed under the British flag the company was seen by the IMMC as becoming something of a liability and in 1927 White Star was sold off to become part of the Royal Mail Steam Packet Company (RMSPC).

Worse was to come. When the RMSPC began suffering in a hostile economic climate, in 1934 the British Government stepped in to offer a financial package that involved White Star merging with its old rival, Cunard. Construction of the *Queen Mary* was already underway for Cunard and plans were well advanced for the building of the *Queen Elizabeth*. So, when the merger went through, with Cunard the senior partner in the new Cunard–White Star Line, the building of White Star's *Oceanic III*, again intended to become the biggest ship in the world, was cancelled. Both Cunard and White Star Line flags were flown on the new company's ships until the late 1950s, when Cunard took over completely. In 1960 the *Britannic* (the third White Star liner to bear the name) was scrapped and the White Star Line was no more.

Cunard continued to operate a transatlantic service, although the nature of the business changed completely. In the years following the Second World War, passenger traffic across the Atlantic was increasingly carried by aircraft, especially with the arrival of the jet age. Cunard's liners such as the *Queen Mary* (now a permanently docked hotel and shopping centre in Long Beach, California), and the *Queen Elizabeth* (destroyed by fire while being converted to a floating university in Hong Kong in 1972) provided an elegant alternative to air travel that was far more of a pleasure cruise than a journey of necessity.

While the *QE II* still crosses the Atlantic, she can just as readily be found during the winter months in sunnier climes where her passengers embark on holiday cruises. This is a far more relaxed way to enjoy a luxury liner than the days when such ships were forging across the Atlantic trying to set the fastest time for the crossing. Cunard's newest liner, the *Queen Mary II*, is the largest cruise ship in the world, as big as a modern aircraft carrier, but entirely devoted to the comfort, wellbeing and entertainment of her passengers.

The *Titanic*, too, was intended to pander to the comfort, wellbeing and entertainment of her passengers but, unlike the *Queen Mary II*, her primary role was as part of a transatlantic shuttle service. The *Titanic* was expected to make money as part of an essential transport link rather than as a floating pleasure palace. The days of transatlantic steamship travel have all but gone. The purpose of the great liners has been reduced to that of a mobile holiday resort, but the modern world's last

tenuous link with the *Titanic* has not yet completely dissolved. The White Star Line has gone, the North Atlantic surface passenger trade has gone, the original purpose of the great liners has gone, but one last link remains.

Built for the specific task of servicing the Olympic-class liners at Cherbourg, the White Star Line tenders *Nomadic* and *Traffic* had working lives that far outstripped those of their parent ships. The *Traffic*, launched two days after the *Nomadic* at Harland & Wolff, was the one earmarked for ferrying third-class passengers from ship to shore as well as transferring baggage and mail sacks. She attended the *Titanic* just once, of course, but went on to serve a useful purpose in the First World War, ferrying troops from their mighty transport ships into Cherbourg from where they would depart for the trenches far to the east.

She continued her civilian duties after the war until her role changed when she was sold to the Société Cherbourgeoise de Transbordment in 1927, after which she serviced any vessel in the port rather than working exclusively for the White Star Line. She was renamed the *Ingénieur Riebell* when the Société was reorganised in 1934. In 1940, as France was being over-run by the Germans during the Second World War, she was scuttled by the French Navy. This effort was intended both to sabotage the port of Cherbourg and to make her useless to the enemy. The Germans, however, raised the *Ingénieur Riebell* and set her to work as an armed convoy escort. In January 1941, she was torpedoed and sunk while serving the Kriegsmarine.

Maintaining the link with the *Titanic*, therefore, is now the sole responsibility of the *Traffic's* sister ship, the *Nomadic*. Like the *Traffic*, the *Nomadic* ferried troops during the First World War and she was sold along with the *Traffic* in 1927, although a condition of the deal was that she should always be made available when required by White Star Line ships at Cherbourg. She was became the *Ingénieur Minard* when the *Traffic* was renamed in 1934, and was involved in the evacuation of Allied troops from France in 1940. After the war, improvements to the harbour at Cherbourg and the decline in the transatlantic passenger trade meant that the *Ingénieur Minard* became increasingly redundant. The last grand liner she served was the

Queen Elizabeth just before she retired to the Far East in 1968. The *Ingénieur Minard* was then sold off and left languishing by her new owner before she again changed hands and had her former name, the *Nomadic*, restored to her in 1974.

She was taken to Paris, having been fitted out as a floating restaurant, and moored on the Seine near the Eiffel Tower for a number of years but again fell into disrepair. She was finally removed to Le Havre to await a fate that is as yet undecided. The neglected hulk of the *Nomadic*, a ship that took shape alongside the Olympic-class liners at Harland & Wolff almost a century ago, remains the last floating link with the building of the *Titanic*.

That last physical link with the *Titanic* may be in danger of crumbling away, but there is little chance that *Titanic* herself will ever be forgotten. There is, in fact, as much interest in the vessel around the world today as there ever has been. The 1996 movie *Titanic*, starring Leonardo DiCaprio and Kate

Winslet, used state-of-the-art computer-generated special effects as well as good old-fashioned water tanks and a 775-foot-long replica of the great liner. The replica, a temporary construction, was 'sunk' so many times during filming that it eventually started falling apart. The movie became the most expensive film ever made, at $200 million, but earned its investors more money than any other movie, too – over $1,800 million! This was, of course, only the latest in the list of *Titanic* movies which include *Raise The Titanic* in 1977, *The Unsinkable Molly Brown* (based on the story of the *Titanic* survivor Molly Brown) in 1960, *A Night To Remember* in 1958, *Titanic* in 1953, a German propaganda film called *Titanic* in 1943 and the very first movie, *Saved From The Titanic*, a silent film released in May 1912, just one month after the disaster. That first movie was co-written by and starred actress Dorothy Gibson, who had been a passenger aboard the *Titanic* and was a survivor of the sinking. The *Titanic* has also starred or featured

Right: The dawning of the jet age cut the time for an Atlantic crossing to a matter of hours rather than days and the era of the ocean liner as an essential means of transport was over. Modern passenger liners like Cunard's Queen Mary II *are now devoted to leisure and pleasure cruises rather than being the most vital link between America and Europe.*

in countless TV shows and been the subject of thousands of books. The whole world watched in wonder in 1985 when video footage of the newly discovered wreck, 13,000 feet down on the floor of the Atlantic, was released by Dr Robert Ballard's survey team. There are successful, and highly professionally run, *Titanic* historical societies around the world, backed up by numerous websites, all dedicated to the preservation of information, photographs and artefacts from the ship. *Titanic* memorabilia, models, illustrations and images are big business. But why is there such a continuing fascination with a ship that was built, and sank, over a century ago?

There are a number of different ways to answer that question. Undoubtedly the age-old motive of avarice has a part to play. Many believe that there are untold riches in jewels, gold and artefacts to be salvaged from the wreck, with various grandiose schemes proposed over the years to raise *Titanic* and recover her treasures. These have all come to nothing and it is highly unlikely that the remains of *Titanic* will ever be moved from the bottom of the Atlantic. There have, however, been a number of attempts to plunder her treasure, although the wreck is now monitored in an attempt to preserve it as a memorial in the same way that sunken warships are protected as war graves.

The idea of treasure under the sea is enough to sustain a certain amount of interest on its own, but there are other sunken vessels that went down carrying valuable cargoes scattered far and wide over the ocean bed. So why does *Titanic* attract so much more attention than any other wreck? Certainly, this has a lot to do with what are often seen as the 'unanswered' questions surrounding the disaster – why the ice warnings were ignored; why there appeared to be every intention of increasing rather than decreasing speed; why more first-class passengers were saved than third class; why the *Californian* failed to respond to the distress rockets; why there were not enough lifeboats or why neither Lord Pirrie nor J P Morgan joined the ship for her first Atlantic crossing. For some people the obvious answers regarding standard practices, arrogance, disorganisation, confusion, possible negligence and the poor health of two elderly gentlemen simply will not suffice.

If there is the merest hint of a blossoming mystery then it must be plucked, savoured and preserved. This has led to bizarre conspiracy theories involving the identities of the *Titanic* and the *Olympic* being switched on the basis that the *Olympic*'s accidents had left her so badly damaged that she was a 'write-off'. On her final repair trip to Belfast, so the theory goes, she was swapped for the new and pristine *Titanic*. The *Titanic*, under the guise of the *Olympic*, then resumed the transatlantic crossings while the *Olympic* was patched up to be sunk deliberately as the 'Titanic' on her maiden voyage so that the owners could make a massive insurance claim. It is nonsense, but the theory does have its devotees.

The real reason why the story of the *Titanic* has endured for almost a century is because of the people involved. The people who built the *Titanic*, the Belfast workers and their families, Lord Pirrie, J Bruce Ismay, J P Morgan and everyone involved with the ship made sure that the whole world knew that this was the biggest, most modern, most remarkable vessel ever to put to sea. She was hailed as the ultimate luxury liner and regarded as 'unsinkable', so her sinking naturally created a sensation that was seized upon by the press. More than that, among the passengers who died were some of America's wealthiest socialites, people whose names appeared regularly enough in print for the newspapers to have a field day. Above all else, of course, was the terrible death toll. For 1,500 people to lose their lives in the accidental sinking of a ship in peacetime is a tragedy of immense proportions. Had the *Titanic* sunk with no casualties, everyone having escaped into lifeboats, none of the books, TV specials and movies devoted to the disaster would exist. Ask anyone what happened to the *Titanic*, where so many died, and they will probably be able to tell you about the ship that struck an iceberg. Ask them about what happened to the *Britannic*, where so many survived, and they won't have a clue.

The treasures that may be on board and the intrigue surrounding the disaster would be enough to sustain a certain level of interest in the ship, but the tales of heroism, forlorn hope and heartache surrounding those who perished and those who survived will ensure that the story of the *Titanic* endures for generations to come.

INDEX